WHEN I WAS A NIPPER

WHEN I WAS A NIPPER

NIPPER

A Personal Journey Through
Disappearing Britain

Alan Titchmarsh

WINDSOR
PARAGON

First published 2010
by BBC Books
This Large Print edition published 2011
by AudioGO Ltd
by arrangement with
Ebury Publishing

Hardcover ISBN: 978 1 445 85930 9
Softcover   ISBN: 978 1 445 85931 6

British Library Cataloguing in Publication Data available

Printed and bound in Great Britain by
MPG Books Group Limited

CONTENTS

INTRODUCTION

Is there any point in nostalgia? I mean, apart from making you feel warm and cosy inside? What good does it do to hark back to days past as though they were times of undiluted joy lived on a diet of milk and honey? And yet *carpe diem* is all very well, but occasionally it does us good to remind ourselves where we have come from and how we have arrived where we are. It puts our lives into perspective, allows us to compare our lot today with the way it was and be grateful for the improvements. Mostly. But there are those little niggles—steam trains and milk with cream on the top—that fill us with a hankering for times past, when life seemed simpler, when dad had a 'gippy tummy' not irritable bowel syndrome, and mum would occasionally retire with 'one of her heads' rather than a full-blown migraine.

I wouldn't want you to think that I am a latter-day Luddite. I'm the first to admit that modern technology is astonishingly helpful. Well, most of it. It has made it possible for man to walk on the moon (though perhaps once is enough), treat a vast range of medical conditions that were incurable 50 years ago and communicate instantly anywhere in the world by email and mobile phone. The prospect of coping with things as they were for ordinary people in our parents' and grandparents' lifetime would horrify the majority of us. Imagine trying to run a home without running water, indoor loos or central heating, without supermarkets stocked with convenience foods, or the vast range of labour-saving electrical appliances and home

1

entertainment that we all take for granted today.

But modern advances have come at a cost. Today everyday life is lived at a faster pace. There is tremendous pressure on all of us to 'achieve'. But in the race to 'better ourselves' we've left behind some of the things we once valued—respect for authority and our 'elders and betters', community spirit, family life and good manners. They were— we thought—the social glue that cemented our society together. They have been replaced, in many instances, by insularity, cynicism and a kind of destructive neurosis. Harsh? Maybe a little, for it is difficult to respect authority, elders and betters when they themselves seem to have forgotten how to behave.

I hesitate to say that things were very different when I was a lad. It makes me sound both ancient and curmudgeonly. But I was born in 1949 and brought up in a Britain that was still recovering from the after-effects of the Second World War. It was a time of relative calm—the nation was getting its breath back after a six-year conflict which threatened its very existence. It was enough for most folk to return home at night knowing that the house would still be standing and that— daily eventualities allowing—the family would be together. The Dunkirk spirit still prevailed, though, since everything from food, clothing, building materials and consumer goods were in desperately short supply. People didn't have television, wall-to-wall carpets or fitted kitchens. Even a fridge and a phone were great luxuries for most folk, and there were still plenty of houses with no mod cons at all.

But we didn't feel hard up—we took it for granted that we must 'make do and mend'. From an early age we would be taught to 'stand on your own two feet', 'look on the bright side' and 'take knocks on the chin'. Well, we did have one vital attribute to see us through; something that no amount of hardship or conflict could quench—our sense of humour. We were known throughout the world for our patience, resourcefulness and resilience—'mustn't grumble' was almost a national catchphrase—and queuing was second nature. But children could play safely outside in the street, families sat down together at a table for meals, and you never needed to lock your doors. A nice cup of tea solved everything (with an extra spoonful of sugar when things were particularly harrowing), and the weather was our big obsession. So what if the winters were freezing and your house had no heating? You woke up every morning to a fascinating pattern of ice crystals left by Jack Frost inside your bedroom window. You dressed quickly and warmly, in thick sweaters and sensible underwear (washed once a week), had a proper cooked breakfast or a large bowl of porridge laced with golden syrup, and didn't feel the cold. Rose-tinted spectacles? Well, only slightly. We might have yearned for an easier life, but we knew it would be slow coming. Churchill's motto applied to us all—KBO—keep buggering on.

But if you've ever struggled to open the child-proof lid on a jar of aspirins, spent a fruitless hour trying to programme your digital TV, or bemoaned the rising price of 'barc essentials' that our grandparents got by perfectly well without, you may—like me—sometimes look back wistfully to 'the old days' when the pace of life was slower, and we had our feet far more firmly planted on the

Me as a baby in 1949.

ground.

Thrifty housewives were the real heroines of the post-war period, but it's incredible how things turn full circle. A good many of 'granny's tips' are proving to be regular recession busters for families today, and a lot of our old ways are making comebacks. Comfort food like steak and kidney pie and good filling puddings such as jam roly-poly are back on pub menus (those pubs that have survived, that is), and fresh locally produced food is on the increase. Long-lasting clothes made of natural fibres are back in fashion, secondhand items are increasingly recycled through charity shops or sold on internet auction sites, and voluntary work in the community or in gardens or nature reserves is a growing trend. Compared to our forebears we are still very much a throwaway society devoted to instant gratification, but maybe some traditional values are reappearing in new guises. It's what happened after the War, and it helped us pull through. Deep down, I suspect, we are just the same

4

people with just the same potential as we ever were. It's just that modern life has blunted our abilities in certain areas. Some of our native aptitudes have been lost through lack of regular use. Perhaps if we remember what we really valued from our earlier years—as distinct from blind nostalgia for times past—we might find a better and more satisfying way forward. Well, it's just a thought. This is, after all, one man's view of what went on and how things were. It may have looked different from where you were standing or where you were born.

TO SET THE SCENE

I was born on 2 May 1949 in the small Yorkshire town of Ilkley in Wharfedale. While not as wild and rugged as North Yorkshire, the West Riding does possess its fair share of beautiful scenery as well as robust industry. Ilkley is one of its more picturesque settlements. The river runs through the centre of the town with Middleton Woods on one side and the famous Ilkley Moor on the other. Ilkley—or Olicana as the Romans had called it—nestles snugly in the valley below the wind-blown heather and bracken. In Victorian times the town had become famous for its healing chalybeate springs, flowing from the moors above. Hydropathic establishments had been opened up to allow posh folk to come and 'take the waters' in the Heather Spa, as Ilkley had become known. But now, in the 1950s, the belief in the efficacy of the waters had waned and the 'hydros' had been turned into ordinary hotels, apart from the largest which had become the 'College of Housecraft'. It seemed to me as a child that nothing much of real import ever happened here. But then all I needed was all around me—woods, moors, a river and a back garden where I could sow seeds and grow plants. Who could ask for anything more?

Ilkley in the very middle of the twentieth century was regarded—along with Harrogate—as a smart residential town for the wool merchants and businessmen of Leeds and Bradford. They lived in the larger, smarter houses up the posher parts of town—streets with names like King's Road, Grove Road and Rupert Road. The rest of us—the plumbers and electricians, the greengrocers and the council workers—lived in rows of terrace houses nearer the station (trains to Bradford, Leeds and Skipton) which nodded at the achievements of inspirational men—Nelson Road, Wellington Road and Trafalgar Road, with occasional recognition of local worthies who all seemed to have been called Beanlands. My mother and father had known each other after a fashion since they were both in their prams. Their mothers were friends and often pushed their charges along side by side, where they exchanged gummy grins (that's the babies, not the mothers) before meeting again more formally some years later. They both went to the same school but only started courting after they met at a dance in the King's Hall—the town's Edwardian assembly room—just after the War in 1946. Dad was a plumber, mum worked in the woollen mill in the nearby village of Addingham. They were engaged within six months, married six months after that and moved in with the mother-in-law while they saved up for a place of their own. They bought their first house in Nelson Road—ten minutes' walk away from Grandma's in Dean Street—four months after I was born in 1949. It was a stone-built terrace property on three floors—two rooms on the ground floor and the first floor plus an attic—and it cost them £400. They bought it with a mortgage.

My sister, Kath, arrived five years later. Since both our parents were Ilkley locals, their parents and their brothers and sisters plus *their* families all lived quite nearby, so I grew up surrounded by aunts, uncles and cousins. We stayed in the same house for 15 years and when we did move—to improve our lot—it was to a pebble-dashed semi on the other side of town. Apart from returning to a different house every evening—and having a lounge *and* a dining room—life went on exactly the same. It wasn't just us; it was how things were at the time. Most folk didn't travel much or move house very often; they tended to stay in their home town close to their extended family, so everyone knew each other, and virtually everyone joined in with the life of the community. Well, there was nothing else to do, and since people worked, shopped and socialized locally, everyone was around in the evenings to take part in things. My family was no exception. Apart from being a plumber, Dad was a part-time fireman; my Uncle Bert ran his grocer's shop by day and a local scout troop in his spare time. Mother stayed home looking after Kath and me, but she was, at different times, enrolling member of the Mother's Union and Brown Owl of the church Brownie pack. The church was not a part of everyone's life, but it did figure largely in ours—though, to be honest, through habit rather than religious fervour. Dad and I sang in the choir, and Mum, Dad and I rang the bells. Kath confined her activities to being one of Mum's Brownies.

My interest in nature manifested itself early on— at the age of eight I was the youngest member of the Wharfedale Naturalists' Society, which met regularly in the Congregational Church Hall in winter to enjoy 'lantern lectures'. In summer there would be evening trips up the Dales to watch birds and seek out wildflowers—each of us crammed into a handful of cars. When I left school at 15, I went to work in a nursery belonging to the Ilkley Parks Department—a five-minute bike-ride away—and apart from family holidays I'd never left Wharfedale for more than a week until I went away to college in 1968 to start my gardening career in earnest. But by then the swinging sixties had arrived, the economy was booming, technical innovations were popping out of the woodwork and life as I'd known it would never be the same again. Nor would it, I suspect, for most other people of my generation. We've had opportunities 'to get on' that our parents and grandparents would never have imagined. But I reckon it does us no harm at all to remind ourselves where we've come from. If nothing else, it helps us keep our feet on the ground.

CHAPTER 1

THE WAY WE WERE IN THE VILLAGE

In the 1950s life was still rigidly structured. Or it certainly seemed so to us. You were either working class (which was us), middle class or upper class, with the royal family at the very top of the social ladder. The working class comprised those people who got their hands dirty. Some of them had aspirations and managed to work in offices, but you could tell that they were not middle class by the streets in which they lived. The middle classes had rather smarter houses—semi-detached, with more than three bedrooms and in the smarter parts of town. The upper classes were detached—socially as well as physically, it seemed to me back then—and lived in big houses with cleaners and sometimes a chauffeur and a cook or housekeeper. People knew their place, and the rights and responsibilities that went with it, and nowhere were conditions more feudal than in villages.

In the 1950s and early 1960s something like half the population still lived in villages, and life was very different there compared to how people lived in towns and cities. In those days the countryside wasn't owned by faceless insurance companies and pension funds; huge acreages were held by titled gentry and large landowning families who'd held their estates for generations. They were regarded with considerable respect since they were the big employers on whom so many rural families depended for their living, but also because, in the main, they valued the contribution made to their livelihoods by those who worked for them.

Even for people who weren't directly employed on the land, the rural economy revolved around villages and the range of thriving local shops and small businesses that were run there, and the village hall was the centre of social life in the community. But living conditions would seem pretty basic to people today (outdoor plumbing was still a common feature of rural cottages), and in *really* rural villages conditions were often not far removed from what they'd been in Victorian times. There is little that's romantic about an outside privy on a cold winter's night. Especially when you discovered that the newspaper as well as the Bronco toilet paper had run out. Loo? No; this is a term not used in the working class parts of Yorkshire until the 1960s. It was 'toilet' or 'lavvy' and none of your posh ideas here . . .

Housing

In towns and cities most homes were connected to utilities such as gas, electricity, water and mains drainage, thanks to all the rebuilding that went on after the War. Not so in the countryside. It wasn't cost-effective to lay pipes and cables through miles of rough lanes and muddy fields to reach a few remote rural properties, so conditions at the most isolated cottages would be quite basic. Farm workers' conditions were the most primitive of all, since they lived in tied cottages that went with the job. As a consequence they were the very last to be 'improved'. To make up for the poor housing and the low wages, farm workers often received other 'perks' such as free milk or firewood from the estate, and the odd brace of pheasant at Christmas, but their wives must have found the housework pretty heavy going without basic 'mod cons'. It was a full-time job, and a laborious one at that.

It was not at all unusual for country cottages to be lit by paraffin lamps, which had to be filled regularly and their wicks trimmed daily to stop them smoking. They were superseded to some degree by propane lamps with disposable cylinders—regarded by some as the height of sophistication. Both types had to be lit every evening if you wanted to find your way about, but they were a great improvement on the candles that had preceded them, not least in that their light was easier to read by. Without wireless and television, reading and board games were a vital source of entertainment. Water had to be fetched in by the bucketful from the well or a pump in the yard, and rugs had to be cleaned by hanging them on the washing line and bashing them with a woven cane carpet beater—it was just as well there were no fitted carpets.

Cottage kitchens were particularly basic. A fridge was out of the question since there was no electricity, so most were equipped with a pantry for storing all the food we'd put in a fridge today. The pantry was a large walk-in larder with a bare concrete or stone-slabbed floor and marble or stone shelves, and it was always built into a north-facing corner, with a small air grille in the wall, so it kept cool naturally. People kept fresh meat in there, under a muslin cover or in a perforated zinc box known as a 'meat safe', to protect it from bluebottles keen to lay their eggs on a suitable food source. Forget to cover the meat in summer and before long it would be crawling with maggots. Milk, cheese and bacon would also be kept on a marble slab.

Because of its size the pantry was also the best place to store home-made jams, pickles and preserves, plus stone jars filled with salted runner beans (alternate layers of salt and sliced beans) and Kilner jars packed with bottled fruit. If you kept hens then any surplus summer eggs would be 'laid down' in a bucket of isinglass (which looked exactly like wallpaper paste) to preserve them for winter when the hens went off lay thanks to reduced daylength and lowering temperatures. There'd be a sack of potatoes from the garden and a box of apples off the tree in the lawn, the fruit individually wrapped in newspaper to keep them in good condition. And since the pantry doubled as a store cupboard, there'd also be a shelf or two for packets of rice, salt and a few tins of peas or canned fruit, just for emergencies. Nothing fancy.

Cooking was done on a coal or wood-burning range—a vast black monster that demanded you were a slave to it when it came to stoking it with fuel. Rising early in the morning and getting it going with newspaper, sticks and coal was the only way to ensure it was capable of cooking food by midday. In winter most folk tried to keep it going overnight by stoking it up with fuel and 'shutting the damper' so it ticked over until morning. It had a cast-iron hotplate for saucepans and stewpots over the firebox, alongside which was the oven— the very devil to use since there was only very basic temperature control, mostly achieved by chucking more fuel on, or opening and closing the damper to regulate the air flow. But farm workers went in for good, plain, hearty cooking so they coped quite well in the circumstances. And when they wanted some hot water for washing up, they boiled a kettle on top of the range. Central heating was non-existent, but if you could keep the range going all the time the kitchen would be quite warm and the doors of rooms left open to circulate the heat.

The sitting-room fire was lit every day in winter and damped down with used tea leaves or damp coal dust each evening to keep it going overnight in cold weather. The wire mesh fireguard with its polished brass rim would be put in front of it for safety, and during the day would be garlanded with damp washing that steamed and fogged up the windows. Some warmth would percolate round the house naturally, but the bedrooms were always cold—there'd be frost patterns on the glass inside the windows on winter mornings. Country people simply put on long johns and warm winter clothes, and when they came in after work in winter they'd pull a long curtain over the inside of their front and back doors to exclude draughts. Just before going to bed, hot coals would be shovelled into warming pans, which were like long-handled frying pans with lids that were slid into the beds briefly to take the chill off the sheets.

Few went to these lengths as late as the fifties. Large stoneware hot-water bottles were the alternative used in our house. Only when they leaked onto the bedclothes did you know that the rubber washer on their stoppers needed replacing. Flat rubber hot-water bottles from Boots the Chemist replaced them. But farmworkers went to bed early during the long dark winter nights, and what with all the manual work, they don't seem to have felt particularly cold even though our winters were far longer and colder back then. In the winter of 1963 the villages surrounding Ilkley were cut off for several weeks by snowdrifts up to 10 or 15 feet deep. Sheep were lost and tractors buried. But come the thaw, life went on as normal, with little hysteria on the part of the farmers.

Laundry was quite an art, without electricity. Monday was the traditional washday; the cottager's wife would start early by lighting a wood fire under the copper boiler in a wash-house which formed part of a range of outbuildings in the yard outside. Clothes would be rubbed all over with a bar of solid green soap—my granny arranged hers under the skylight in the attic so that it would become harder and longer lasting. It would be used in strict order—the one that had been there longest was used first. Once the water was up to temperature the washing went in to 'stew'. After a while it was prodded around with a wooden 'dolly' or 'peggy stick'—a four-legged stool fixed to the end of a pole—which was pushed down and twisted so the clothes were well-pummelled to loosen the dirt. Eventually new technology brought the 'posser'—a dome-shaped copper device with holes in it, also fastened to a pole. It was used to push the washing up and down in the tub of hot, frothing water.

Since it took ages to heat the water, you used the same lot over and over again for everything, starting with the cleanest things first and leaving dirty working clothes till last. Filthy farming overalls would be given a good bashing outside with a stiff yard broom to detach the worst of the mud and muck first. As each load of laundry came out

16

of the now scum-laden 'copper' it was put through an old-fashioned mangle that you turned by hand to wring out the water, then collars and cuffs and other areas needing special attention would be given another dose of green soap and rubbed hard against a washboard—a sort of short corrugated tin plank stood on end over a sink—before being rinsed and put outside to dry. Everything was pegged out on a long clothes line outdoors, and raised up into the wind by the clothes prop—a long forked pole with a notch cut in the far end. Anything that still felt damp at the end of the day was dried in front of the kitchen range or the open fire in the sitting room, hung over the top of the fire guard or a wooden clothes horse.

Tuesday was ironing day. A pair of heavy metal flat-irons were stood on an iron trivet over the sitting-room fire or on top of the kitchen range to heat up, and a huge wooden ironing board set up nearby. When you were ready to do some ironing, you lifted an iron off the stove by its handle (using a folded cloth to prevent your hand being burned), and to test the temperature you spat on the flat surface. If it sizzled that was the signal to go ahead, and then you ironed as quickly as possible; you knew the iron was too cool for the job when it no longer ran smoothly and easily over your linen, so the iron went back on the stove or

A very modern pressure iron—there weren't many of these in Ilkley.

17

over the fire and you switched to the second one which was still heating up. Fabrics in working-class dwellings were very hard-wearing and robust. They had to be. Socks with holes in (known in our house as 'taters') were not thrown away, they were darned by mum of an evening. She would insert the large wooden darning 'mushroom' into the sock and, using a pattern of crossing stitches in a wool that might, with any luck, match the original colour, would fill the hole and give the sock another few months of life.

The lack of bathrooms is what always strikes modern families as the worst hardship, but arrangements were really quite cosy. Every bedroom had a large china bowl and jug (ewer) on a table; you'd heat a kettle of water on the range and carry up the freshly filled ewer to fill your basin for a 'strip wash' in your own room. The idea was to wash *down* as far as possible, then *up* as far as possible. At least, that's what people said at the time. As for the weekly bath, you brought in a tin tub from the outhouse on Friday night and sat it on newspapers arranged over the rug in front of the living-room fire, then filled it with hot water from several kettles and all the biggest saucepans heated over the kitchen range. It was a slow process, and the tub had to be topped with more hot water halfway through, which meant having a helper on standby in the kitchen. After all this effort it was regarded as a waste to have only one bath, so the family would be cleansed in order—the children being popped in last of all. When Mum and Dad installed a proper bath in the attic at Nelson Road, Grandma would come round once a week for a 'proper bath', leaving her tin one to gather cobwebs

18

ever after in the shed in her backyard.

With no indoor toilet, there'd be an outdoor privy down the yard, which again had a unique atmosphere all of its own—complete with ivy growing through knotholes—and if you left the door pushed open a chink with your foot you could watch the sunset of an evening. Toilet paper was rough, like greaseproof paper, replaced by squares of newspaper when it ran out. And on frosty winter nights? Simple; people had a chamber pot—a 'gazunda'—beneath the bed, to be covered by a square of cloth for its journey through the house in the morning, and emptied down the privy.

Things often weren't all that much better at the 'Big House' (as the local landowner's manor or farmhouse was known) or even at the rather more modest properties lived in by local worthies such as the doctor and the parson or vicar. Oh, they had more rooms, and they were larger and more comfortably furnished, but they were still cold and draughty with few facilities. But being better off, people who lived in big houses employed local women to come in to do the cleaning and laundry, and local men to come in and do a bit of gardening—and when mod cons became available, they were the first rural homes to have them. The rural rich also had cars so they could travel to nearby towns for stores and provisions that village shops didn't stock—but their lives were still remarkably circumscribed.

The local community

The local community was virtually your entire world if you lived out in the countryside. But almost everything you needed could be found in the village, and everyone helped each other out in times of trouble. People were far more self-reliant in those days, and they needed to be since there was a lot less help—and less interference—from the State. Since rural communities were small, everyone knew everyone else, so rebellious youths seldom dared step out of line. They knew that word of any misdemeanours would soon get back to their dad, who'd 'deal with it'. Usually this amounted to no more than a whack on the bum with the flat of the hand, though really severe cases were reckoned to warrant a few well-placed swipes with his thick leather belt (worn in addition to the braces) or, in my own case, with a whalebone hairbrush. It's a state of affairs that provokes horror today. I can't say I'm in favour of it, but I don't feel emotionally damaged as a result of the couple of times it happened. For minor misdemeanours like scrumping apples or on 'Mischief Night'—the night before Bonfire Night—when we'd knock on doors and run away, the local bobby or indeed any adult-on-the-spot would take matters into their own hands, and a swift clip round the ear would be instantly administered. The same held good in small country towns, too, as I and my friends knew to our cost. Everyone felt that was as it should be; the ear-clipper would only have been doing their public duty and would not end up in trouble themselves, as so often happens today. One of the things that seems to have been lost over the past 50 years is the capacity to feel ashamed. There's a lot to be said for the salutary effect of humiliation, but politicians have done their best to disprove that.

A typical village had several thriving shops

concentrated around the centre. The largest of these was usually a general store, selling provisions and fresh local veg, newspapers, sweets and possibly a few pots and pans and essential haberdashery—needles, cotton, balls of wool, elastic and the delightfully named and seemingly essential 'bias binding'. The store was often combined with the small sub-post office, which had a counter for stamps, postal orders, parcels and pensions. If a stranger arrived in the village, the general store was the first place they'd go for directions if they were lost, since the person behind the counter always knew everyone and everything. Today we call it being a busybody. Come to think of it, they did back then, too. The village store was invariably the hub of village news and gossip since everyone went in there at some time every week.

Near the general stores you'd find a couple of other essential village shops: the butcher's and the baker's. The butcher didn't stock trays of ready-cut, shrink-wrapped meat; he was a craftsman who bought live animals from local markets, probably slaughtered them himself in a shed out the back using a humane killer, and then butchered the carcase. Crossing the floor of his shop, sprinkled with sawdust, the better to absorb the blood, he'd cut meat to order from a side of beef, pork or lamb hanging on a hook from the ceiling of his shop, chopping it off with a hatchet on a huge wooden block, and then trimming or boning it with a wickedly sharp knife. The Big House and other local worthies generally bought the expensive roasting joints, while cottagers had the cheap bits, the mince, scrag end, offal, pigs' trotters and even the head. Every bit was used. The bakery started

*The village relied on a well-stocked
corner shop.*

work early since they baked their own bread on the premises, and they'd be selling it still warm from the oven each morning. The choice was not large—you could have brown or white, all unsliced, made in tins or long tubular 'bloomers' with pointed ends and seeds stuck on top; sometimes there'd be rolls as well as loaves, and on special occasions they'd make fancy shapes such as cottage loaves. All were wrapped in tissue paper for their journey home—paper that eventually found its way into my album of pressed flowers to prevent the pages sticking together.

The local doctor was nothing less than a God. Referred to as 'Doctor'—without the definite article—his word was law. He (it was rarely a 'she') would often hold his surgeries in a room set aside at his own house, otherwise he'd have a practice in rooms that were converted from a shop or house near the village centre. It was quite an informal arrangement. Surgeries were held morning and evening, and at least two village spinsters would vie for his attention, whether he was married or not. Prospective patients turned up without an appointment, checked in with the receptionist—who was often the doctor's wife— and then sat in the waiting room till their turn was called. They could sit there for hours, but it was a great opportunity to compare ailments with any neighbours who you met there or to read the stock of well-thumbed glossy magazines that were kept on the table especially. It was the only way most villagers ever read the likes of *Horse and Hound*, *The Field* or *Country Life*—generally at least a year out of date.

Anyone who was too ill to come to the surgery would be visited at home, outside surgery hours— even in the middle of the night—in an emergency. This necessitated the house being cleaned from top to bottom in advance of his arrival, were the housewife anything like as good as she should be. Doctor would palpate your chest with his icy fingers and bring to bear a stethoscope of equal coldness. You would say 'aah' a lot and apologise for being a nuisance. Anything really serious and you'd be sent to the cottage hospital, in the nearest small town, within easy visiting distance for your relatives. A rural doctor may not have had a large number of patients, but he looked after them all himself and knew every detail of their ailments—you only saw a stand-in if he was taken ill himself or went on holiday.

The pub was a vital part of community life— every village had at least one, and if it wasn't situated in the very centre it would certainly be within easy walking distance. People didn't go to the pub to get drunk but rather for a sociable evening out, and since all the locals knew each other a convivial time was assured. Pubs had two separate entrances, one leading into the saloon bar and the other into the public bar. You couldn't wander into the wrong one by mistake, because the name was written on the door. The saloon bar was reasonably well decorated and furnished with seats and tables, but you'd only go there if you were well dressed. It wasn't just the preserve of 'toffs'; ordinary married couples would smarten up before going to enjoy a night out together—he in a suit and tie and she in a dress and a tailored coat, perhaps with gloves. He would have a pint of bitter, she a schooner of sherry or, if feeling particularly sophisticated, a Babycham (champagne perry) or a Snowball (lurid yellow egg-nog frothed up with lemonade).

The public bar might have sawdust on the floor and rough-hewn wooden benches, but that was the centre of social life for working men, who didn't need to dress up. They might drop in for a pint and a game of skittles, darts or dominoes at the end of the day, and you were likely to meet local characters who'd stopped on their way home with a couple of dead rabbits or a gundog. There'd often be a piano, and locals would have a sing-song— there was no canned music in those days. Round the back of the pub—or through a hatch from the public bar—was the off-licence, where you could buy beer to take home in bottles or, cheapest of all, you took your own jug and had it filled from a barrel. Nowhere else sold alcoholic drinks; except for dedicated off-licences, who also sold bottles of spirits and fizzy drinks. In those days soft drinks and beer were sold in returnable bottles; you'd get a penny or two back each time you returned your empties. It was one of the best recycling schemes ever devised, since the original supplier simply washed and refilled the same bottles, without melting them down. It also provided small boys with a source of income since they had a good incentive to find and return empty bottles for pocket money.

The pub also ran a Christmas Club, which was the way rural workers put money aside for a few festive luxuries. People would pay a little into their account every week, or each time they dropped in at the pub, then in December they'd collect their payout in good time to spend it on turkey and presents. But what pubs seldom provided was food. There might possibly be a thick doorstep of a sandwich, but few bar snacks or meals and certainly no separate restaurant. In fact there were no family facilities of any kind—rarely even a garden with tables and chairs. Nobody under-age was allowed inside licensed premises. If a couple went to the pub on a Sunday lunchtime they'd leave the children outside and perhaps send out lemonade and a packet of crisps or pork scratchings. And pubs were still very male dominated; unaccompanied ladies wouldn't have gone into one alone—and certainly not into the public bar—for fear of being thought less than perfectly respectable if not actually 'fast'. My grandmother died aged nearly 90 in the late 1970s and still proudly boasted that she had never been into a pub. Mind you, she made a lethal sherry trifle.

Licensing hours were quite short, a few hours at lunchtime and again from after work until ten every evening—slightly later at weekends. As each session drew to a close the landlord would call 'last orders' indicating that you had about ten minutes left to get your last drink, then he'd call 'time'. You were officially allowed ten minutes drinking-up time before you had to leave the premises. Oh, the odd rural landlord would stretch a point sometimes, or he'd close the doors and allow his friends to continue drinking later, but the local bobby would drop round regularly and make sure licensing laws were being obeyed. I mean, you never knew what out-of-hours drinking might lead to . . .

Further out from the village centre was the village hall, and what a powerhouse this was. A place where the Women's Institute (the WI) met, where Friday night dances were held and the local amateur dramatics group rehearsed—they'd occasionally put on plays and entertainments over the year, and there'd be the pantomime at Christmas. They were always well supported since everyone knew the entire cast, and anyway there was nothing much else to do. In some cases the village hall doubled as the school hall, gym and dining room for the local primary school. And around election times the local candidates would hold meetings to address the electorate, and they'd usually have a goodish turn-out. Well, if somebody important like that took the trouble to turn up it was thought 'only polite' to turn out and listen to them. Even if half the time you took what they said with a pinch of salt.

The vicarage in those days was a huge, rambling, cold, draughty old house with large reception rooms and enormous grounds with a spacious lawn. Since vicarages went with the job they were

26

tied houses of a sort, but they were considerably grander than those of farm labourers since their house and gardens were expected to double as venues for church functions. During the year most villagers would visit several times for church garden parties, fêtes and other fund-raising events, and mothers' meetings and choirboys' teas took place regularly through the summer. The church was usually very close to the vicarage and had its own social life, what with bellringers, the choir and flower-arranging rotas. Most village families took an active part in church affairs, and they turned out for all the big church festivals and celebrations over the year.

Harvest festival was always a huge event in rural communities where most people earned their living off the land, so you'd see massive piles of produce stacked up all round the altar, donated by local farmers and householders with large vegetable gardens, and bakers made huge loaves shaped like sheaves of corn—everything was given away to local hospitals and 'homes' afterwards. Easter always saw the church traditionally decorated with white lilies, and at Christmas it was all berries and greenery (but no mistletoe since it was considered pagan). Even Christmas trees were regarded with suspicion by many local clergy—fine at home, but not in God's house.

Sunday school was held on Sunday afternoons for children too small to sit through normal church services, and took place in a little room round the back of the church, or else at the village hall or maybe in the rectory, depending on numbers. The Sunday school I attended was presided over by the vicar's wife—a gnarled little lady with grey hair scraped back into a bun. I can't admit to ever finding it stimulating, but it gave us a good grounding in basic Church of England beliefs and traditions, and from there we were expected to graduate to family services. It wasn't just for the deeply devout. 'The Church' was 'a good thing'— guaranteed to give a child a good start in life and to help it recognize right from wrong. It stopped kids from 'hanging about' and getting into trouble— and it gave parents a few hours off from parental duties. Words like 'nativity' and 'resurrection' were part of our everyday Sunday life. We would learn the parable of 'The Sower' and 'The Widow's Talents', be told bible stories, and would eventually be introduced to the church service and the *Book of Common Prayer* with a language that would offer its own peculiar kind of solace. I cannot claim to have been hugely enamoured of church services in my childhood, but even at the age of eight or nine I did get more comfort from the response to 'The Lord be with you' when it was 'And with thy spirit' than I do now from 'And also with you'. We sang in church the Te Deum and the Nunc Dimittis, the Venite and the Magnificat. We might not have fully understood everything we said, but we would have been unlikely to have perpetrated the solecism made in one recent primary school's scripture lesson. 'On hearing that she was the mother of Jesus,' wrote one pupil, 'Mary sang the Magna Carta.'

The primary school in those days was within easy walking distance of most rural homes. Classes might be small and conditions rather basic but it did the job—even if a good few farm workers' sons went mysteriously absent at harvest and other times of peak workload. From the age of 11, children had to travel further to school, often cycling several miles with satchels on their backs. They were very lucky if there was a bus service, unless they lived on a main route between towns—a lot of villages didn't have any public transport. But all children did a lot of walking; it didn't do them any harm. We were all fit, slim and active, and there was only ever one fat boy in the class—a state of affairs inevitably attributed to 'his glands'.

Rural employment

Farming was still a huge employer of manpower (of which more later), but farm work wasn't the only job for the men in rural communities. The countryside was used for all sorts of sports and activities which between them generated lots of work for the locals.

Hunts were big employers. Every area had one of its own. The large fashionable hunts in 'the Shires' (especially Leicestershire) were said to provide the best sport since that particular patch of countryside provided a challenging range of fields to gallop over, fences, hedges and ditches to jump, besides copses and woods where foxes could breed in spring, then use to go to earth during the hunting season. These hunts attracted people up from London for weekends in the hunting season— and real enthusiasts also hunted midweek—so there were lots of jobs for locals looking after the small weekend homes used as 'hunting boxes', not to mention grooms in livery yards, as well as the hunt servants and the kennel staff who looked after the hounds. They'd also employ a terrier man—

usually a local farm labourer earning a little pocket money—who kept the Jack Russell terrier that was put down foxholes to flush out the inhabitants if they went to earth too soon. Less prosperous areas often had their own 'farmers' hunts', mainly for the tenants of small local farms and their families, but even these generated a few jobs since they still needed to maintain a pack of hounds.

Hunting has a very dubious press today and no longer takes place in its traditional form, but 50 years ago it played a big role in country life. It was—and some would argue it remains—the most important way of controlling foxes. Most farms, smallholdings and cottages kept a few hens running round their yards, so a resident family of foxes could greatly lower the standard of living for country families, besides depriving them of a good little income-earner if they sold surplus eggs at the garden gate. Sheep farmers worried about foxes taking their new-born lambs, and gamekeepers were very well aware of the damage they could do to populations of ground-nesting birds such as pheasants and partridges, so landowners were generally keen supporters of hunting—and they'd usually ride to hounds themselves. But the hunt also did a good deal to manage the countryside. Farmers were encouraged to leave hedgerows and small copses, which provided cover for foxes, when in other parts of the country land was generally being cleared to make better use of tractors and large combine harvesters.

Stiles, fences and ditches were also well maintained on land that the hunt ran over, since suitable obstacles made for a better day out. The hunt also played an important role by removing what were known as 'fallen stock'. Farmers didn't send for the vet when a cow became crippled, when a sheep fell sick or a horse broke a leg—they sent for the huntsman, who'd humanely despatch the poor beast and take the carcase away to feed to the hounds. The hunt also had a big social side. It was one of the ways the sons and daughters of the aristocracy could meet 'the right sort of people', and a lot of relationships that began caked in mud in the bottom of a ditch or looking for a runaway horse in the woods were continued over a stirrup cup in the squire's front garden before the next 'off', and finally took root at the big Hunt Ball that ended the season.

Early each autumn the new hunting season started with 'cubbing'. This was the name given to the first few informal outings at the beginning of the season when the hunt servants chased a few of this season's young foxes around a bit to train the new crop of young hounds. The idea was to send them out with experienced older hounds to learn the ropes—they didn't want them to be distracted and end up chasing rabbits or cats—but it also gave the horses a little light exercise to start getting them fit after they had spent summer out at grass getting fat. 'Cubbing' was also popular with children, novice riders and newcomers to the sport (who wanted to get a few outings under their belt without much of an audience in case they fell off, or fell foul of hunting etiquette), though a few locals on ponies would come along for the ride. It wasn't a time for serious enthusiasts, who saved themselves for the start of the proper hunting season which went on through the winter. The big outing never to be missed was the Boxing Day Meet, which, as well as the regulars, attracted the great and good of the county in their full finery. Hunts also organized point-to-points, which began life as informal races, organized by rival horse-owners, across country from one church to another in the next village, taking every natural obstacle in their stride. Gradually—one suspects as the horses grew too valuable to risk on unknown, potentially hazardous, ground and landowners objected to thundering hooves cutting up their fields of growing crops— they moved to small local racecourses where they were run over thorn hedges.

Wherever you had a hunt, you needed a blacksmith. Most villages of any size had a smithy. The forge was run by a brawny man wearing a thick leather apron who spent the day tending a fierce fire next to his anvil, where he'd usually be found bashing away with a huge hammer at a piece of red hot iron or nailing a shoe to the hoof of a huge horse tethered to a ring in the wall. It was a good, reliable rural trade that country mothers were keen for their sons to go into, since besides shoeing horses, it was the blacksmith's job to mend farm machinery, make gates and undertake any fancy wrought-iron work. He was always busy, all year round. And given his size and build—which were both impressive—nobody argued with him. His smithy would reek of coke and smouldering hoof in equal measure, and the perspiration would run down his brow as he cradled in his hands the mighty limbs of the local horses.

Pest control provided another source of good regular rural employment. The rat-catcher and the mole-catcher would be regularly sent for by farmers and owners of large houses. Even the doctor or vicar might send for them to clear out infestations on their property. Moles might seem pretty harmless, since people weren't generally that worried about maintaining immaculate lawns, but it was a disaster when moles invaded livestock pastures. If cows or horses—especially valuable hunters—put a hoof down a mole hole and broke a leg, there was no saving them. Riders often took nasty tumbles, too, when galloping across fields riddled with mole runs, so the culprits were firmly dealt with. The mole-catcher was an expert on mole movements and behaviour; he'd poison them using worms soaked in strychnine, which were placed down mole runs, or would trap them using underground devices rather like miniature gin traps set into their tunnels. (Today poison is banned and you can get humane mole traps that catch them alive.)

If you'd visited the village pub you could usually tell a mole-catcher straight away by his moleskin waistcoat. Well, you couldn't eat moles, but there was no need to let their velvety coats go to waste. There was also a market for moleskin to be made into collars for jackets; what made it so sought-after was that besides being short and glossy-black, the fur could be stroked in any direction—just like velvet—because a mole often needs to go backwards in its run as well as forwards. The rat-catcher had no such perks. He'd use big strong wire traps or he'd take his terriers to catch the rats and shake them to death. Rats would ruin stored grain and root crops, steal chicken feed and take birds' eggs from pheasant nests, as well as breaking into cottages and contaminating human food supplies or nesting in thatched roofs

33

and spreading disease, so really they couldn't be tolerated. Most cottagers kept a few rat traps of their own even if the estate they worked for used the services of the rat-catcher. You'd often see them hanging up on unused nails in their shed.

Oh, life in the countryside could be hard, but it was full of local colour. And if you've been reading this and you live in a village, there will have been moments where you will have said to yourself, 'well, it's still like that'. Of course it is. But the city dwellers will wonder what on earth you are on about.

CHAPTER 2

THE WAY WE WERE AT THE SEASIDE

For any boy or girl not keen on school, holidays were the light at the end of the tunnel—be they at Christmas, Easter, Whitsuntide or the height of summer, they represented freedom pure and simple. Not that they were organized holidays—except for, perhaps, one week in summer. No; the other holidays were for 'playing out'—kicking a can around in the street, playing hide-and-seek, cricket or football against the bus garage wall with chalked up goal posts or wicket, lighting fires in an overgrown back garden and hoping the fence didn't catch fire and other such blameless pursuits. Once you'd helped your mum out with the washing up or swept the backyard, you were a free agent for the day. It meant, in my part of the Yorkshire Dales, that you could go up on the moors to the paddling pool or the tarn, down by the river or across the swing bridge into Middleton Woods where bluebells carpeted the ground in late spring and ropes could be hung from branches to facilitate Tarzan impersonations.

The 'proper holiday' was not something enjoyed by every family, and you certainly didn't expect one every year. You got a week in summer if you were lucky—I was well into my twenties before my first fortnight's break, and even now I find that length of enforced idleness rather a trial. How my father—a plumber on a very basic wage—managed to afford to take the four of us away to the seaside for a week

35

is still beyond me. And that's where we went—for the first 15 years of my life at least.

Virtually everyone had their holidays in England back in the fifties; it was almost unheard of for 'ordinary folk' to go abroad until foreign package holidays took off in the mid-1960s, and then they were usually to Spain. Mrs Walkinshaw from the chip shop was the first to go. My mother was very dismissive. Mrs Walkinshaw had no teeth, and the fact that she put sunshine before dentures was something my mother could never forgive.

I was rather more impressed by the Lambert family. They lived 'up The Grove' and their father was something in Leeds. Wore a suit. (Mind you, in those days my dad wore a sports jacket and a tie under his overalls so that the folk whose ballcock he was mending could see that he had made an effort.) The Lamberts went to Majorca, as he kept reminding us. Not for a week, but for ten days. They came back a strange shade of orange, and I assumed that the sun was somehow different out there.

Before such exotic destinations became de rigueur, many families opted for a tension-packed stay with relatives in a different part of the country. We didn't have any relatives my mum wanted to stay with, so off we went, with the rest of humanity to the seaside. The larger mill towns up north had 'Wakes Week' when all the workers were given their annual break. The result? Packed trains, belching smoke from their engines and taking the workers to the coast for a week of sea air, sand and seagulls, warm beer and cold water. But what a time we had! We'd book into boarding houses or holiday camps, which were the big new thing. The

There was a whole host of opportunities for holidaymakers taking a well-earned break from the daily grind.

countryside hadn't been 'discovered' as a holiday destination. Well, it was just like home for most of us, and where was the fun in that? Posh folk might have gone hunting, shooting and fishing, but we knew nothing of them, and there was no such thing as a 'city break'. Who in their right mind would want to be cooped up in the smoke? Oh no, if you wanted a proper holiday, best get off to the seaside.

Seaside resorts

The most popular resorts were the grand old Victorian and Edwardian seaside towns such as Blackpool and Brighton and Hove. You went, as a rule, to the one your family had always gone to, though up north these tended to be the closer resorts on the Yorkshire and Lancashire coasts, or Wales for the really adventurous. The Lamberts, up The Grove, went to Devon and Cornwall before they discovered the delights of Majorca—but these were far too distant for us to contemplate. It would take you half the week to get there. Well, a couple of days anyway, and that ate into your week—especially with another two days taken up at the end fighting your way back through Indian Queens.

The choices for us were fairly limited. Blackpool was a bit common, Morecambe was for the oldies, and Lytham St Annes for those who thought themselves a bit above the rest. It was quiet and select: i.e. boring. Those that could afford it stayed in the grand hotels that had once made those towns famous with the upper-middle classes, but most of us stayed in boarding houses. There were hundreds of them, scattered down side streets behind the prom with evocative names such as 'Buona Vista' and 'Seaview' (whether it had or hadn't), 'Bay Cottage' and 'San Remo', though farther away from such an exotic location it would be harder to get.

Large, and even modest-sized, private houses, festooned with net curtains, rented out rooms by the week, with a shared bathroom on every floor and a communal lounge where residents could listen to the wireless or watch TV in the evenings (which was quite a treat in the days when you didn't have one at home). There would be a bookshelf in the hall stuffed with the well-thumbed works of Georgette Heyer and Edgar Wallace, John Creasey and Agatha Christie, and often a jigsaw puzzle half completed on a baize card table in the 'residents' lounge'. The accommodation was clean but basic.

Today's B&Bs are positively luxurious by comparison; now it's all en suite with tea-making facilities and a TV in your room, and a rack of tourist information in the hall. Everything is several degrees smarter—even the geraniums in the window boxes look glossier, but we've rather lost the feeling of being temporary members of a seaside landlady's extended family for the week, and nowadays week-long bookings are rarer than they were—it's a night or two here and a night or two there. Shorter attention span you see . . .

The big treat for Mum was that she didn't have to cook for a week. The dining room of 'Pendennis' in Hesketh Avenue, Bispham was not large. It held, perhaps, three or four small tables and seated around eight or ten holidaymakers. Breakfast and 'evening meal' were served between restricted hours. You missed a meal at your peril—if you'd booked 'full board' there were no refunds for meals not taken. Most people booked half board, since it was cheaper and more fun to eat out at lunchtime. And anyway, I think the Schofields drew the line at cooking lunch, though they could, at a pinch, provide sandwiches wrapped in waxed paper, along with a packet of Seabrook's crisps, a chocolate marshmallow and a bottle of pop. The evening meal was not of the adventurous sort. Curries were, as yet, something my dad had only eaten under duress during his time in Bangalore during the War. They were not something anyone would *choose* to partake of. Dad was happier with Mrs Schofield's pies, boiled potatoes, chops, liver and fish on Friday. That did us nicely, along with lots of sliced white bread and butter and a cup of sweet tea. Puddings were all served with custard.

The biggest drawback to boarding house holidays was that you usually had to vacate the premises during particular hours, however dreadful the weather, to allow the lady of the house to go about her business unfettered by guests. But it was a small price to pay. Seaside landladies became the watchword for clean, economical accommodation. Some of them ran their establishments with a clockwork efficiency that bordered on military operations, but there were lots of lovely ones who endeared themselves to all and became family friends to whom you returned year after year, and never departed without leaving a small thank-you present—a knitted toilet-roll cover, perhaps, or a novelty telephone pad.

After a cooked breakfast every morning— fortified with only a snack lunch in prospect—we'd sally forth with everything we needed stuffed into Mum's basket including our pac-a-macs, a regular essential against the driving rain.

SAUCY POSTCARDS

The one thing you always had to do on holiday was send postcards. It was partly good manners and partly a gentle reminder to let the rest of your family or social circle know that you'd been away. Lucky you.

Although there were plenty of picture postcards with scenic views of sandy coves and the Blackpool Tower, the sort that we kids liked best were the saucy Bamforth comic illustrations with curvaceous blondes with alarming bosoms straining out of tiny bikinis, rosy-cheeked spherical ladies in vast swimming costumes and short, gormless men with bald heads and moustaches. We understood some of them; others left us in the dark, but in the end my mum would settle for a picture of the Tower to send back to Grandma and Auntie Alice. Still, on wet afternoons you could while away many a merry half-hour round a saucy postcard stand at a beach-front kiosk. Nowadays the originals are collectors' items that turn up at antique fairs.

If only Mum hadn't settled for that view of the Tower . . .

But there was glamour, too. Mum always took at least one good home-made dance dress so that she and Dad could go out of an evening and have their Fred Astaire and Ginger Rogers moment waltzing round the Tower Ballroom. While they had their Friday and Saturday night out dancing or at a show, they'd put Kath and me to bed after a glass of milk and a biscuit and leave us in the care of the boarding-house proprietors. Oh, I know today that would be quite out of the question, but in those days it's what everyone did; since you went back to the same place every year you knew the owners very well—they were almost adopted uncles and aunts to us.

During the day—or at least the days when it didn't teem with rain—we spent our time on the beach, with our picnic of sand-filled egg sandwiches and bottles of Vimto or Dandelion & Burdock (a special treat instead of the usual lemonade, though mum drew the line at Cream Soda which, she said, rotted your teeth). From ten in the morning to four in the afternoon we engaged in the traditional seaside tasks of building sandcastles or larking about in the sea. Grandma Titch—Dad's mother— spent her annual week at Morecambe where she largely spent her time playing bingo. She found that more profitable than sitting on a beach. Her generation was not one that sat in the sun—it did your skin no good at all and you ended up looking like a farmhand. As a result she became a dab hand at whist and very lucky at bingo, judging by the bags full of prizes, mostly rainhats, she came home with. Still, they must have been one of the more sought-after objects, considering that a typical summer back then was two days' sun followed by one of thunderstorms—the northwest-coast resorts enjoyed more than their fair share of wet.

Entertainments

At least on holiday we had the opportunity to do all those things we couldn't do at home. Holiday resorts

42

had a huge range of facilities for enjoying yourself, and since you had a whole week off from normal everyday life the whole family was free to devote themselves exclusively to having fun. There was no holding back—people really threw themselves into a traditional bucket-and-spade holiday. Any halfway decent seaside resort had lots of cafés, funfair rides and theatres. Along 'the front' were stall after stall selling candyfloss and Blackpool rock, cowboy hats with 'Kiss Me Quick' on the front and 'Hug Me Slowly' on the back. There were beach balls and windbreaks, shrimping nets, buckets and spades— tin at first, plastic when the world went modern— all dangling temptingly from striped awnings at the front of shops that never seemed to have an inside just a weather-beaten man or woman standing in a doorway and unhooking whatever you wanted before you made your way to the beach.

Blackpool also had a tiny zoo, with a real live (if rather mangy) lion, and the Tower Circus, with Charlie Cairoli, the red-nosed clown with the bowler hat, and the white-faced, saxophone-playing Paul in the sparkly costume and the pointed white hat as his stooge. Most holidaymakers would divide their time between the beach by day and these other amusements in the evening or when it rained. Buy your ticket for the Tower Circus, and the high spot came at the end. When the lady had swung from the trapeze and dropped gracefully into the safety net, when the clowns had got their come-uppance with custard pies and the lions had roared and been tamed, the entire circus ring sank down and water poured into it. The grand finale was a spectacular cataract of fountains, illuminated by coloured lights. And then you got up and traipsed back wearily to the boarding house, wondering just how they did it without flooding the ballroom.

The beach, though, was the big attraction; all the most popular resorts had wide sandy beaches and shallow bays that were safe for swimming— and where the water warmed up quickly as the tide came in over hot sand. We'd take a picnic with us to the beach and would spread out our rug, packets of sandwiches, Thermos flask and bottle of pop, and settle down for a serious session. We were easily entertained; not for us the wetsuits, surfboards, stunt kites and barbecues that modern families find essential for a quiet day on the beach. A canvas windbreak would have been the height of sophistication. We only had my dad, and he was on the slender side.

A popular holiday beach would have deckchairs for rent—the old-fashioned sort with canvas seats and folding wooden frames that collapsed at the first opportunity, especially if someone kicked the vital strut that held your weight. Some places also had rows of beach huts which were either owned by families and used every year or rented out by the council for the week to use as changing rooms and for storing your picnic stuff. On wet days they were handy for sheltering from the rain—you could sit and read your thriller or romance, or peruse the paper with a flask of tea while you waited hopefully for the sun to come out, or simply nod off secure in the knowledge that no one would wake you up and tell you it was time to go to work. What you couldn't do was sleep in your beach hut overnight. So no one did. Well, not respectable folk, anyway. If anyone had told us that, 50 years later, beach huts would be swept along by the property boom

44

and become valuable investments, changing hands for £30,000 or so in desirable locations, we'd have thought they'd had a touch too much sun.

Larger resorts had donkey rides up and down the sands—a dozen or more tired animals that were on auto-pilot when it came to the route. Tiny tots had to be held in the saddle by a parent each side, though the attendant simply walked alongside older children—they weren't going to come to any harm since, no matter how hard you kicked, a seaside donkey could never be coaxed into anything faster than a slow shuffle. Long queues would often form for the pleasure of a taste of the Wild West—this was the nearest my sister and I got to horses. Kath and I were regular patrons of Nellie and Sampson on Blackpool beach. We knew their names as they were painted on their bridles, and a ride along the sands was all part of our holiday ritual. Today, beach donkey rides are a rare novelty, only available at a few top resorts. When the donkeys on Margate beach retired in 2008 after 120 years (different donkeys, one hopes) they were front-page news.

There might be a Punch and Judy show, with the same familiar characters and storyline that we all knew by heart; we'd sit spellbound, cross-legged on the sand, waiting for Punch to clout Judy round the head with his lump of wood, for the baby to fly out over the edge of the booth, and for the policeman, the string of sausages (what *was* their relevance?) and the crocodile to put in their appearances.

But the one thing you had to do at the beach was make sandcastles—you could pass hours with your brightly coloured little beach bucket and spade, so long as you took care not to cut your feet on the sharp metal edges. You could

45

make a simple castle by piling up damp sand and patting it into roughly the right shape with the spade, but a real enthusiast would add turrets by upending buckets of well pressed-down sand and decorating them with little paper flags on sticks— Union Flags, red lions of Wales, harps for Ireland and the Saltire for the Scots—hoping all the time that the whole lot wouldn't collapse before the structure was completed. A really superior sandcastle would have a moat dug round it, which you tried to fill with water by running back and forth into the sea to fill the bucket, before it all ran away, and if you were really artistic you'd decorate your edifice with seashells. Some resorts held sandcastle competitions, and a few kids (who one always suspected cheated by getting their dads or older brothers to help) made the most fantastic fairy-tale creations before the incoming tide washed them away—slurping them into oblivion and clearing the beach for another day's creativity.

But by far the best thing to do at the beach was to bury your father in sand—by piling it up over him as he lay dozing, leaving just his head sticking out. He'd wake up and feign crossness at being made a fool of. At least, we always hoped it was feigned. It was less risky, perhaps, just to dig a huge hole for the fun of watching it fill up with water as the tide came back in.

If the beach had a suitable rocky outcrop we'd go rock-pooling, hunting for crabs and generally seeing what small fish, shrimps or seaweed the tide had left behind. There'd be limpets and mussels clinging to the rocks and several different sorts of seaweed. You'd take your shrimping net and, picking your way carefully over sharp and slippery rocks, bewigged

46

by green weed, dredge the depths to pull out some small, unfortunate sea creature. Go to the boating lake along the prom and you could catch the crabs by tying a broken-open mussel to the end of a piece of string. Some of them were huge and would scuttle back into the water with a plop before you could summon the courage to pick them up.

Collecting shells was another big seaside-holiday must, and even a plain sandy beach could yield a good harvest. Kids would see how many different kinds they could find, and then take them home to use as free craft materials for making seashell pictures or sticking onto the lids of wooden boxes— but mostly they just cluttered up our bedrooms until mum said they were nothing more than a dust trap and threw them out.

The one thing you didn't really do at the beach was sunbathe. Well, you might lie back for half an hour to warm your bones, but we didn't really go there to get brown. Even parents tended to cover up when they weren't actually swimming to avoid getting burnt. Suntan lotion? Well, mum would have some Nivea in her bag if your skin got a bit dry. Bald men would make themselves sunhats by knotting the corners of a large white handkerchief and pulling it over the top of their heads, which made them look just like the comic characters in the saucy postcards. Men had trunks which were more like shorts, and I was kitted out in the same sort of grey knitted woollen swimming trunks that all small boys had at the time, which absorbed a good deal of salt water and sagged alarmingly when you walked out of the sea after your dip. Their only concession to fashion was a maroon fillet down each side—a sort of sink-faster stripe. Ladies wore shapeless one-piece garments—sometimes with a frilly skirt to hide the tops of their thighs—that they'd top with a most unflattering rubber swim hat to keep their hair dry when they went into the water. For sitting around they'd usually throw a towel round their shoulders or pull something loose and smock-like on—quite often you'd need a sweater, and it wasn't unusual to see adults swathed in rugs behind canvas windbreaks swigging tea to keep warm on cold windy days. Well, you were on holiday, so whatever happened you were doggedly determined to make the most of it.

But the most fun of all, at resorts that had one, was the pier, since that was where all the serious seaside entertainments were centred. The end-of-the pier entertainments were where you found funfair rides such as the big dipper, dodgems and roundabouts with wooden horses that went round and round and up and down, but there'd also be the ghost train, the hall of mirrors, and a motley assortment of fortune tellers and penny-in-the-slot machines, plus the inevitable candyfloss stalls. Half the fun was watching the vendor dip a short wooden stick into a vat of spinning sugar strands and seeing them build up into a big sticky dome like a bright pink beehive hairdo. The result took some eating, especially in a high wind, and left you feeling faintly sick, but it was one of those things you had to do when you were on holiday. Somewhere on or near the pier there would usually be a bandstand, where the 'oldies' could sit and listen to the music—usually a fairly robust brass band, which was the only thing that could compete with the background racket caused by holidaymakers having fun. Then at the very end of the pier—or in the centre of town if there wasn't a pier—was the theatre. 'Summer season' consisted of popular shows featuring the likes of Ken Dodd or the Black and White Minstrels. All the big names would appear. And a holiday wasn't a proper holiday without going to see a show of some sort.

Running parallel to the beach, between the sea and the town, was the promenade. The 'prom' was the vital link with all the other seaside attractions— you might dress up and walk along it of an evening to see and be seen, or continue along it and onto the pier on your way to a show. The teenage girls that you'd noticed walking by during the day with their Teddy-boy boyfriends—their hair in curlers held in place by pink or pale-blue net— would walk along the prom in the evening with their hair combed out into a beehive or flick-ups. Their lads wore draped coats of blue or maroon and black suede crepe-soled shoes known as brothel creepers—their own hair Brylcreemed into a DA with a shiny quiff at the front. The girls' dresses would look like something off *Strictly Come Dancing*, with layers of pastel-coloured tulle billowing out from beneath a fitted bodice and stiletto-heeled shoes off which they would occasionally tumble. The transformation was hard to believe. But then, as the evening wore on, and the Babycham and Cherry B began to take its toll, the hairdos would become more unruly under the 'Kiss Me Quick' hats, and the language more raucous and colourful as they sloped off home, occasionally throwing up in the gutter. They'd reappear the following morning, bleary-eyed but curlered once more in preparation for another night on the tiles.

A large town might have trams running along

the seafront as well; they usually had open tops so that anyone fit enough to fight their way up the stairs while the vehicle was moving could enjoy panoramic views. On wet or windy days the top decks were conspicuously vacant, and the trams would warn you of their approach with a crack of electricity and a shower of sparks from the overhead wires as well as the customary clack of their gongs.

At places like Lytham St Annes the promenade led to the golf links, but there were usually facilities for those whose handicap was more to do with lack of finance. Crazy golf involved an hour or so spent chipping balls into a series of little houses through the open front door and out the back. Or, for frustrated mariners, there was the boating lake where for a small sum you hired a rowing boat or even a very slow motor launch bearing a number which would be called out by the attendant if it wasn't handed back on cue. 'Come in number 9, your time's up,' they'd bellow through their loud hailer. No response. 'Number 6 are you in trouble?' My dad loved that one.

All along the prom were great formal beds of annual flowers laid out in traditional carpet bedding much as they'd have been planted in Victorian times. For me they were one of the highlights of any seaside town. I marvelled at the floral clock, with the face laid out in blooms and hands that (usually) really worked. You'd often see huge floral displays planted up on roundabouts, round the original marble horse trough, or statue, or the big town clock. There was always something jolly to see, and what made it so special was that there was nothing the least bit like it back home. After all, that's why you went away. Very few big seaside towns go to such enormous lengths today; well, it must cost a fortune. Eastbourne is one of the last places you can see traditional seaside floral displays on a grand scale. But today big seaside towns are not just about sun, sea and shells. In winter they welcome the suits—Brighton, Bournemouth, Eastbourne and Blackpool today enjoy a thriving conference season. Now, nobody mention Punch and Judy . . .

Package holidays

As more people started to have regular summer holidays, and holidays grew longer, the idea of booking your accommodation, travel and maybe even meals and entertainment all in one go looked very attractive. 'All-in' package holidays quickly caught on—with one visit to the travel agent you could make sure everything was taken care of.

Holiday camps were brilliant for families with young children—everything you needed was safely inside the camp enclosure, so there was no need to go outside at all. You could eat yourself silly, swim, sleep, join in games and competitions, go dancing, take part in beauty contests or talent shows, all for no extra expense, so you knew exactly where you stood. Only your drink would have to be paid for and your morning newspaper. The big advantage for parents was the childcare facilities which meant they could leave the kids and spend some time on their own or go out in the evening without worrying about babysitting. 'Baby Crying in Chalet Number 132' the sign at the side of the stage would flash, and some embarrassed parent would shuffle out of the auditorium and back down the avenues of

51

chalets to number 132 to comfort the wailing infant.

Unlike boarding houses, you were free to use your accommodation 24 hours a day if you wanted. Mind you, it's not as if there was much in it to entertain you. We certainly didn't have a telly in ours—just bunk beds for us and a double for mum and dad, plus a curtained wardrobe and a washbasin. There were baths at the end of the block. We tried Butlin's at Filey twice, largely I think because Dad found the prospect of sixty quid a week all in for the four of us irresistible. All four of us—me, Mum, Dad and my sister Kath— were crammed into that one-roomed chalet which, to give it its due, bore a striking resemblance to a large garden shed. I'm told they've come on a long way since then. The thing everyone who went remembers about Butlin's was the Redcoats who acted as combined babysitters, big brothers and sisters, and events' organizers. They were responsible for everything, including running the camp tannoy system (though mum was relieved to discover that they did not get you up in the morning with the 'Wakey-wakey, rise and shine, time for another nice day at Butlin's' that she had been expecting).

But Redcoats were, to my eye, hugely glamorous. They performed in shows and acted as masters and mistresses of ceremonies for everything from the Bonny Baby to the Glamorous Grandmother, Mr Debonair and Knobbly Knees competitions. A lot of young people found the job was a useful way of earning a bit of extra money during the holiday season, but it also acted as a spring-board into a career in variety shows, and for some it really paid off; quite a few well-known show-business

52

personalities began their careers as Redcoats: Sir Cliff Richard, Des O'Connor, Isla St Clair and Jimmy Tarbuck among them.

Coach holidays were a bit like holiday camps on wheels. As kids we'd had the occasional one-day charabanc outing organized as a special treat for the church choir and their families, but when the likes of Wallace Arnold came along they made it possible for people without cars to visit far-flung parts of the country, stay for a week or so, and be taken out seeing the sights every day. Some of them had the atmosphere of a working man's club outing, with singing and beer, and frequent 'rest stops'; others were more 'select'—depending a lot on their destination—but choose the right one and you could be sure a good time would be had by all.

Once the British public had developed a taste for holidaying 'all found', the way ahead was clear for reasonably priced package holidays abroad. (Package foreign holidays certainly existed when I was small; Thomas Cook had started sending wealthy clients off on organized trips abroad before the War, but in the fifties they certainly weren't for ordinary working folk.)

Spain was the first popular destination, and for a lot of people it was the first time they had been exposed to strong sun, strong drinks and foreign food. I didn't go abroad at all till after I was twenty. Well, Mum was nervous about the idea of foreign travel with two children in tow—you never knew what might happen, and tales from people she knew who'd been didn't help put her mind at rest, so we stuck with what we knew best: Blackpool. But for those who did take the plunge, Spain was an absolute eye-opener, and it had a huge influence on all sorts of everyday life back home. People who'd previously only eaten regulation, medium-sized, round, red tomatoes where aghast when confronted by the Spanish ones, which were enormous, ugly, contorted great brutes with green shoulders and yellow lumps, but once they'd discovered how much better they tasted, people started to demand them at home—and if they had a greenhouse, they wanted seeds so they could grow their own as well as the traditional old favourite, 'Moneymaker'.

People began to decline a bottle of light ale and drink wine with their meals, and not just when they held a dinner party for the boss and his wife and wanted to appear cultured by producing a bottle of Bull's Blood or Blue Nun. And once they'd discovered foreign food was not going to kill them or leave them with gippy tummies, people started to be slightly more adventurous with things like pasta—previously only found in tins with the name Heinz above the picture of spaghetti in tomato sauce.

But for me the most noticeable side effect of all those Spanish holidays was on our gardens. Holidaymakers had seen small enclosed paved Spanish gardens decorated with gaily painted tin cans planted with geraniums, and with a grape vine on a pergola overhead to cast shade over the table and chairs where the owners sat outside for meals on hot days. Suddenly everyone wanted something just like it at home. They came back and turned the backyard into something they'd heard called 'a patio' and that's when the great container gardening craze started. It's been going strong ever since.

THE RISE OF THE HOLIDAY CAMP

The idea of holiday camps had started between the wars when there was a great health and efficiency craze which brought families out on do-it-yourself camping holidays under canvas, but development was halted by the hostilities; few people were able to take holidays, and the camps were often taken over for military accommodation.

By the time the last war ended everyone was desperate to get away for a cheap seaside holiday, and, although the conditions were pretty spartan, holiday camps came on in leaps and bounds, with chalet accommodation and communal buildings, and by the 1950s there were hundreds at seaside resorts all round the country.

There were three big holiday- camp groups:

- Harry Warner opened the first of his camps at Hayling Island in 1932.

- Billy Butlin opened his first camp at Skegness in 1936, and people could have a week's holiday for a week's pay, an ideal arrangement for working people. Clacton came next, and then Filey in Yorkshire— where we went. Butlin's camps were far bigger than others, usually holding around 2,000 guests at a time, compared to the usual camp site that held a few hundred, so they were able to offer a greater range of entertainments and activities.

- Fred Pontin appeared on the scene in the late 1940s, but he went in for much smaller camps advertised as 'for the connoisseur', taking under 250 campers at a time.

CHAPTER 3

THE WAY WE WERE ON THE MOVE

Travel was something of a luxury when I was a lad, and most people didn't wander very far from home. Apart from the annual family holidays to Blackpool, until the age of twenty I'd only left Wharfedale on a few odd day trips, and I wasn't the only one. There was simply no need to go far. Neither was there much money to spare. Most people worked within walking distance of home or just a short bike or bus ride away. Their relatives lived close by, and school was within easy walking distance—by the time you graduated to senior school, even if you lived in a village, you still only needed to go to the nearest big town. That was about as far as most people normally went for rare shopping excursions or an occasional trip to 'the pictures'. Few people owned cars, so the roads were virtually empty. My dad's first van—a bottle-green Austin A50 pick-up provided by the plumbing firm he worked for—arrived in 1960 and was just about the first in our street.

There were no huge articulated trucks or refrigerated transport because nothing much needed to be hauled around the country—there were no supermarkets and a relatively restricted range of consumer goods. Food was either produced locally or it came by rail to a local depot where it was decanted into a small van that made deliveries to local shops. It was just as well since even the main roads were more like today's country lanes. Dual carriageways were rare (we had a little bit—about half a mile—between Ilkley and Skipton) and motorways hadn't been thought of. Long distance travel took *hours and hours*, so most people only bothered with it for their holidays.

Public transport

The most glamorous form of public transport, in my youth, were the Bradford trolleybuses which had replaced the old trams. London had them, too. Trolleybuses were like huge double-decker buses powered by electricity via two big antler-like rods running up to overhead power cables, and as they moved—especially in wet weather—they showered sparks all over the roof. In a good downpour it was like a mini-fireworks display. Naturally trolleybuses had to stay close enough to their power lines for the rods to reach, so cars had to keep out of their way. That was bad enough, but driving in cities such as Leeds, Bradford or London in the 1950s was a real obstacle course because the roads were still rutted with the old tramlines, and if you got the narrow tyres of your fifties motorcar stuck down the narrow channels you could end up missing a vital turning before you could escape.

There was nothing like today's traffic congestion in London—the roads seemed quite empty. There were very few pedestrian crossings, bollards, roadworks or one-way systems, and cars could park along the side of the road, even in places like Oxford Street and Regent Street—but even so trolleybuses soon proved too much of a hindrance. They were gradually phased out in favour of the familiar red double-decker Routemaster buses with the open rear deck where the passengers got on, which had completely taken over by the 1960s. But trolleybuses certainly gave London streets lots of character—that and all the dazzling neon signs that lit up advertising hoardings around theatreland and Piccadilly Circus. As a lad I only went to London once—on a scout trip. I marvelled at Big Ben and Piccadilly Circus, with the traffic circling Eros, but I was quite glad to get home. All that noise and bustle. But it was good to say that you'd *been*. I felt positively sophisticated.

In cities and big towns, red buses were the main way of getting about; they ran frequently making it easy for people to get to work, shops or schools and in the evenings to go out to theatres and cinemas; with so few cars on the road, buses were what everyone used for getting about. In Ilkley we had a choice of two bus services—the scarlet-liveried West Yorkshire Road Car Company, and the blue and grey buses of Samuel Ledgard, a private company who ran their own service. They were renowned for the smartness of their private-hire coaches, but also for the spartan nature of their public buses—old tickets and fag ends spilling out of the litter bin alongside the rear platform. Smoking was upstairs; non-smoking down.

Services were a good deal rarer in the countryside. Rural routes had Green-Line buses, which were single-deckers since they needed to fit under all the overhanging trees and low bridges. Some places had a regular service every half an hour, running between two big towns and calling at every village on the way, but some remote villages might have one or two buses a week, usually coinciding with market day in the next big town. As for school buses, there weren't any—you got yourself to school on regular bus services, by foot or by bike. Some rural pupils cycled 10 miles to and from senior schools every day—others were brought from outlying moorland villages in a Dormobile—an early, compact version of a minibus. No wonder we were all slim and fit.

Railways

For the best part of a century, until the early 1960s, Britain was tremendously well served by its railways. Then, in 1963, Dr Richard Beeching, the Chairman of British Railways, published his report on 'The Reshaping of British Railways'. It cost anyone who wanted to buy it £1 from Her Majesty's Stationery Office. It cost everyone in the country rather more dearly than that. By the end of the decade the railways had lost approximately 6,000 miles of track and 3,000 stations. Until then, almost every town of any size—and even large villages—had a station, and you could get to almost anywhere from anywhere else, as long as you had a timetable and didn't mind making several changes. What's more, at the end of your train journey you could be fairly sure of finding a bus waiting to take you to your final destination, since public transport was very much more 'joined up' in those days. It was what we used to call 'efficient'.

There were 'stations' and 'bus stations'. Nobody called a station a 'train station'. That would be like calling a baker's a 'bread baker's'. Only the bus station was so designated to differentiate it from the one served by trains. It's a small point, but one that drives me barmy . . .

Not surprisingly, trains were the way most

people travelled when they had a long distance to go and when going on holiday; boarding school pupils used the train to come home for the holidays and to return next term; and virtually anyone in 'professional' jobs travelled to work by train from the suburbs that were multiplying all round cities. Commuters could easily be recognized by their 'uniform' of double-breasted suit, collar-and-tie, twinkly polished shoes, briefcase, bowler-hat and an immaculately rolled-up umbrella which I'm sure most of them never used. Oh, and a newspaper. *The Times* mostly, or the pink *Financial Times*. Those wishing to make a statement about their independent views would read *The Guardian*. When I was older I detected a gratifying number of commuters reading *Amateur Gardening* on the train. Nice that. But you could forget comfy, casual clothes, trainers or 'dress-down Fridays'—formal wear was the order of the day, all day, every day.

Trains were great fun to travel on and also to watch. It was still mostly steam trains when I was growing up. The first diesel, while a thrill on the first encounter, quickly palled. Where was the bit that drove it? One end looked exactly the same as the other, and there was no smoke to run through when it went under the footbridge. On long-distance trips we might be lucky enough to see what trainspotters called 'namers'—famous trains with evocative names on brass plaques, such as *Mallard*, *Sir Nigel Gresley* or *The Flying Scotsman*. There were specials like *The Cornish Riviera Express* or the *Brighton Belle*. These big intercity steam trains were the jumbo jets of their day, carrying 1,000 passengers with very few stops and proper sit-down dining cars with several sittings for meals;

Railways need steel—
steel needs railways

ALL the way along the line (so to speak!) British Railways work in full collaboration with the Iron and Steel industry. Special trucks have been designed for the delivery of raw materials to the works; others for the delivery of finished iron and steel from the works. In fact, British Railways are always ready to consider designing special wagons for carrying any material in bulk.

From cars to caraway seeds

There is nothing British Railways cannot transport and everything is dealt with as a separate problem. For instance, bicycles, chemicals, furniture have special facilities; perishable goods have highly insulated containers—the most efficient of their kind in Britain.

Near-express speeds at night

Most of the freight work is done at night when the lines are quieter. And now more and more freight trains are being fitted with vacuum brakes. Not only does this make for greater safety it also means trains can run at near-express speeds, and so increase line capacity and improve punctuality.

Whatever your product, whatever your problem, you can rest assured that British Railways will give you excellent advice and first class service. Just get in touch with your local Station Master or Goods Agent and your transport difficulties are over.

➡ **GREEN ARROW SERVICE** Operating for both overseas and certain home freights in full wagon loads, this service enables you to register consignments all the way to the destination station or port for only 2/6d. Ask your local Station Master or Goods Agent for full details.

Steel plate unloaded by magnetised grab.

A special wagon for this exceptional load—a depropaniser 128' long.

BRITISH RAILWAYS

The railways relied on the British steel industry, and vice versa.

The Flying Scotsman could do King's Cross to Edinburgh in six and a half hours—an incredibly short time in those days. When I came down to London for my interview at Kew Gardens in 1969 it took four and a half hours from Leeds City to King's Cross.

The *Brighton Belle* was a fast London-to-Brighton Pullman service. It was all first class with nice little tables and lamps between the seats, and posh dining cars with five-star silver service. The day our family travelled down to Southampton in the 1950s to visit Dad's best man, we discovered that the engine that pulled our set of carriages on the Leeds to London leg of the journey was *Mallard*, and my street cred rose enormously with the trainspotting set at school.

Railway carriages were divided into several small compartments, sometimes opening onto a corridor by a sliding door, but often not—thus leaving toilet arrangements rather up in the air (or more commonly, in the case of unaccompanied schoolboys, out of the window). There were all sorts of 'special' compartments: first class (six seats per compartment, with armrests between them), second class (eight seats and no armrests) and third class (not very comfortable, rather like cattle trucks with seats, but usually only on short suburban routes). There were smoking and non-smoking areas, and occasionally you'd still meet a 'ladies-only' compartment with a green label on the window designating it as such, though by the nineteen-sixties the sign was largely ignored.

Carriage interiors were generally cosy and well upholstered, decorated with adverts for worthy products. 'What are laxatives?' I asked at the top

63

of my voice on one journey, to the considerable embarrassment of my mother. Or there would be framed sepia photos of some exotic destination such as Dawlish Warren or Newquay, intended to whet your appetite for further rail travel. Panelling was of exotic woods—deep blood-red mahogany or orange-brown timber, even in second class. Windows could be lowered using a thick leather strap whose holes were anchored to a brass stud, but in practice they were rarely left open more than a crack because if you opened one fully and put your head out into the slipstream you'd get a face-full of smoke and smuts.

People would pass the time quietly on long train journeys, usually dozing, daydreaming or watching the countryside go by to the rhythmic clickety-clack, clickety-clack, or they might bring pocket chess sets or solitaire, in little travel cases with folding lids. Small kids would be given colouring books and crayons and expected to sit quietly for the duration. Running around and screaming would never have been tolerated and any parent with boisterous children would have been most embarrassed if they'd made a nuisance of themselves or disturbed fellow passengers. Oh, it was all very peaceful. When we went on holiday or to Leeds for the day by train, Mum and Dad took a little reading matter to pass the time—light romances for her (Ethel M. Dell was a guilty favourite) and Westerns for him. My sister and I would have comics to read—Kath had the *Swift* or *Robin*, and I'd usually be given the dreary *Children's Newspaper* which wasn't much fun but was considered more educational than average. I'd usually manage to lose it before the return trip, so then I'd just have to settle for a copy of *Hotspur* instead. Heigh-ho, happy days.

Just about every small boy wanted to be an engine driver when I was growing up; well, at least half my class at school did, including me. It was my great ambition to take charge of a shiny mechanical monster belching smoke and hissing steam, to be able to use all the levers, knobs and valves, and blow the whistle. I often tried to hop up onto the footplate to take a look in the cab when we travelled by train but I was always told firmly 'it's not allowed', so I'd have to satisfy myself by snatching admiring glances at the cowling, paintwork and copper pipework from platform level. Besides the driver, each train had a soot-blackened, sweaty fireman who shovelled coal into the roaring boiler, and a guard who blew his Acme Thunderer and waved the train off at stations. The guard also checked the tickets, working his way from one end of the train to the other making sure no third-class customer was sitting in a first-class seat, or presumably vice versa. A railway-mad schoolboy would happily have taken his pick from any of these highly desirable jobs when he left school—but once steam trains were replaced by diesels, everyone's enthusiasm evaporated; the romance had gone.

Back in the days of steam, even waiting for a train was an experience. Every station had a large crew, and the station's flower beds would be tended by the keenest gardener in the team. Flower beds would be edged with white-painted stones—bedecked with wallflowers, polyanthus, daffodils and snapdragons in spring, lobelia and alyssum in summer. Hanging baskets brimful of bloom would dangle from the serrated edge of the platform canopy—a throwback to the designs of Sir Joseph Paxton in the middle of the nineteenth century.

The stationmaster was the top dog, in charge of everything, with a uniform that let you know he was boss. In the ticket office there'd be someone to sell the tickets—not just tickets to travel, but also platform tickets so you could go out to the train to see someone off (I seem to remember they cost 2d). There'd always be someone sweeping up, or watering the geraniums in the hanging baskets. Large stations also had ranks of porters to help people with their luggage and find them taxis in return for a small tip. Even quite small stations had a waiting room so passengers didn't have to sit in a draught and be peppered by smuts while waiting for their train, and larger stations had ladies-only waiting rooms. Oh, it was all very proper. What's more, in winter, waiting rooms had a fire that was kept burning all day using lumps of coal blagged by junior porters from the firemen of trains that pulled up alongside. Everything possible was done to make the traveller feel cared for, and you could set your watch by train services—they always arrived and departed bang on time. Regardless of leaves on the line or the wrong sort of snow.

Trainspotting

Trainspotting was the favourite pastime for any train-mad small boy, and despite a mounting list of outside interests, even I had a go. I was never as passionate about it as some, but I still managed to tick off plenty of train numbers in my book. To the uninitiated—especially today—it must seem like a strange and inexplicable pastime, but this is how it worked.

First you needed the sets of little books (Ian Allan's ABC series) listing all the various types of engines, coaches, engine sheds and their numbers; between them these made up the 'enthusiast's bible'. You also needed a notebook small enough to fit into your coat pocket, plus a packet of sandwiches and a bottle of pop. At weekends, you'd take all this lot with you to a suitable station or a level crossing where you could watch passing trains. You might go to one of the London main-line stations if you lived near enough or from Ilkley, take a train to Leeds and buy a platform ticket. There you'd note down the number of every train, its destination (from the boards on the platforms) and the number that was found on a little metal disc on the front of the train or emblazoned on its side next to the driver's doorway, from which you could look up (in one of your little books) the engine shed it was based at. Sometimes you'd be lucky enough to spot a set of carriages being pulled by an engine that came from outside the region or you might spot a goods train that was an unusually long way from its home shed, and if you asked the signalman he'd be able to tell you why that was. Occasionally, a mechanical problem meant they'd had to bring in someone else's engine, so you'd have a bit of history to stow away in your notes. You soon got to know all the other trainspotters in your area, and it was all very competitive. Other kids would ask what you'd seen. Rare sightings were the holy grail of trainspotting; you could brag about what you'd seen or sell the information on to other trainspotters for as much as sixpence.

Oh, it all sounds a bit dull now, I know, but there really wasn't all that much else for lads to do at the time, and it offered a chance to experience the collecting bug at very little cost. Lots of my friends were completely obsessed. To this day there are elderly gents who still keep their old trainspotting notebooks up in the attic, as keepsakes, and a fair number of old steam trains have been restored by enthusiasts. Steam lovers can once again take a short trip by steam train (the Watercress Line in Hampshire, the Bluebell Line in Sussex and the Keighley and Worth Valley Railway in Yorkshire, for instance) and at some centres fans can pay for a day's 'footplate experience' and see what it was like to be a real engine driver.

Of course, the lucky ones are those who get to drive the trains regularly in their retirement. They may have waited a long time, but in the end their childhood dreams really did come true.

Horse-drawn transport

Incredible though it seems now, there were still a few horse-drawn vehicles around in the 1950s and 1960s. Some breweries still used horse-drawn drays for transporting kegs of beer to pubs, and in London the tradition continued quite late because the accountants worked out that heavy horses (usually shires) were the most cost-effective way to make deliveries in busy streets crowded with slow-moving traffic and where the pubs were relatively close together. Young's and Watney's drays were a familiar sight; their liveried draymen would hold up a big whip to stop the traffic while the horses pulled out of their yard and onto the street. Even today, long after they stopped being economic for deliveries, brewery drays can still sometimes be seen putting on displays at agricultural shows all round the country, since most of us love the sight of these magnificent animals in their huge collars and harnesses, decorated with highly polished horse brasses, pulling elaborate carts. They make good on-the-hoof advertising, and sales no doubt soar in the beer tent.

But drays weren't the only horse-drawn vehicles on the roads. Round the outskirts of London you'd see shaggy ponies pulling ramshackle carts belonging to 'rag-and-bone men' who looked just like real-life versions of Steptoe and Son. I'd often see them after I'd started my stint as a student at Kew. They were continuing a valuable recycling role that started during the War, by salvaging unwanted metalwork for scrap and buying and selling second-hand furniture. Consumer goods were still in quite short supply for a long time after the War ended, so scrapyards were a good source of odds and ends, and—so people thought—there was always the chance of finding a valuable antique that had been overlooked. No chance—rag-and-bone men weren't daft.

Nineteen-fifties Ilkley had its own familiar horse-drawn vehicle. It belonged to Mrs Briggs, who was our very own lady pig-farmer. She drove round town with her pony and trap collecting food waste in the half dozen huge metal dustbins that she kept in the back. She dressed like a bag lady, and the ripe aroma that trailed in her wake made her more than usually . . . distinctive. (Wouldn't be allowed nowadays, of course; feeding swill to pigs has been banned for many years because of the foot-and-mouth risk.) We also sometimes saw another great local 'character' who rode around Yorkshire towns on a huge horse, selling copies of the book that he'd written himself, from a supply that he stashed in his capacious saddlebags. William Holt would dismount in the centre of Ilkley, by the fountain, and flog a few copies of *The Wizard of Whirlaw* before moving on. I found one in an old bookshop a few years back and felt obliged to buy it, from a sense of nostalgia.

In the suburbs just about anywhere in the country you'd still see occasional horse-drawn milk floats. A horse that knew the ropes was worth its weight in gold to a chap with a busy round; once he got off the main road and turned into the leafy avenues he could get off and shoot up and down front paths delivering Pintas here and there, while the horse slowly ambled up the road to keep pace with him, snatching a mouthful of grass off the verge or a bit of shrubbery overhanging a garden wall. And very popular milkmen's horses were, too, with householders who had rose beds in their front gardens. Many's the time you'd see a sweet little old lady in dressing gown and curlers rush outside with her delicate little drawing-room coal shovel in her hand to collect up the latest steaming pile left outside her house to spread round her flowers. I feel rather a killjoy telling you that fresh horse manure (especially while it's still at body temperature) is generally thought far too 'strong' to put round plants, but it seems in this instance a little of what they fancied did them good, because roses always flourished where milk deliveries came by pony-power.

Your own set of wheels

If there was one thing any boy needed, growing up in the 1950s, it was a bike. You relied on it to see friends, get out and about, and go to school. But you couldn't start out on two wheels—your first steps to independence came under strict parental control in the backyard, with a three-wheeler. Small kids were given a Tri-ang tricycle, or 'trike', with solid tyres. Once you'd mastered that, you moved on to a 'fairy cycle'—a small two-wheeler with stabilisers to keep you upright, but you naturally tried to get shot of the training wheels as soon as possible because they marked you out as a 'cissy'. Once you'd found your balance and could be relied on to travel a reasonable distance without falling off and knocking your front teeth out (a common hazard for overconfident beginners) you'd graduate to a small 'proper' bike, and upgrade to larger models as you grew bigger, till you could manage a full-sized grown-up one.

Naturally a brand new bike was an almost unheard-of luxury for most families, so the same old second-hand ones would be passed on round all the relatives, including distant cousins, until they virtually fell apart. Girls had bikes, too, but their version didn't have a crossbar, and the back wheel was fitted with a spoke guard so that it could be ridden with no loss of modesty by someone wearing a skirt, without the fabric getting jammed in the spokes or mud splashing up her backside. You wouldn't have caught a lad dead on one—he'd have sooner walked.

The time to splash out on a brand new bike was

71

when you started work and were earning your own money for the first time—a great moment in a lad's life. Fifty pounds (an enormous sum) bought you a Raleigh or a Humber. A lot of men still used a bike to go to work, and for those who had a long distance to go from home it wasn't unknown for them to cycle to the bus stop and leave their bike in a nearby friend's shed during the day, to be collected for the journey home. But as soon as they could afford it, most thrusting young chaps wanted to trade up to a motorbike.

Their first step was often a motor-assisted bike, a sort of beefed-up bike frame with a tiny engine attached so you could use the pedals or the motor. Then came the moped—perhaps a Honda 50—named after the 50ccs of its engine. It was almost a motorbike but not quite. And then there was the motor scooter—a Lambretta or a Vespa. In the mid sixties they would become the province of the Parka-wearing 'Mods', as opposed to the leather-clad and hairy 'Rockers', but in the 1950s motor scooters were the transport of the sedate or the elderly, like my Uncle Archie.

Real motorbikes were the sort of grown-up boys' toys every lad aspired to. There were lots of British makes, largely collectors' pieces now: Triumph, Ariel, BSA Sunbeam, AJS and Matchless, and Norton; the BSA Bantam (painted duck-egg blue) was the bike used by telegram delivery boys. Being a whole lot dirtier, noisier and faster, a motorbike was naturally far more macho, but riding it wasn't the end of the fun. Most motor-bikers spent their weekends taking their pride and joy apart and tinkering with the innards, spreading oil and spare parts all over the front garden—or the rug by the

PETROL

There was no brand-name petrol until the mid 1950s, when it cost about nine pence a gallon. And that's old pence (240 of them to the £), and imperial gallons (roughly 4.5 litres)—the equivalent of about 4p a gallon.

Then along came adverts. Suddenly we had Esso, whose familiar slogan promised happy motoring, endorsed by the beaming family always pictured in their roadside posters. You could have three grades: Regular, Premium or Extra—the best, costing slightly more, was for posher cars with fancier engines. Woe betide anyone who economized and put cheap low-grade petrol in performance engines because it caused 'pinking', which was clearly not something a driver wanted—not least because it gave away his penny-pinching habits to the passengers in the back. Shell went in for a system of one, two or three stars instead. What appeared on the little window on their pumps looked more like cockleshells, more in keeping with the company name.

The price of petrol rose to a dizzying 1/7d (8p) a gallon and then up to a seemingly impossible 2/3d (11p) a gallon, but it stayed there for some time before creeping steadily upwards again. Garages also sold 2-stroke, for motorbikes and lawnmowers, though a lot of owners made their own by mixing oil and the cheapest grade of petrol in a can and shaking them up together, then decanting the result through a funnel.

fire in the front room to the horror of their mums. Well, as they no doubt explained, they had to do their own repairs and maintenance since they couldn't afford to pay someone else. But things changed as soon as they acquired a girlfriend or wife. She did not care much for getting her hair messed up sitting astride a motorbike behind the 'driver' so, if a car was out of the question, they'd add a sidecar for taking her—and later the kids— out in at weekends. The entire ensemble was cheap to run since you still only needed a motorbike licence, which only cost about £6 per year compared to a car licence which was twice that. And sitting in a sidecar was very cosy, especially in iffy weather.

'But what about safety?' worried mothers will by now be wondering, and with good reason. Few motorcyclists wore helmets at the time. It wasn't compulsory; lads liked the feel of the wind in their face and, in any case, to wear a helmet suggested that you expected to fall off, which meant you must be a rotten rider. To create a suitably rakish image, macho motorcyclists would wear a cloth cap back to front, so the peak was at the back, with a pair of ex-RAF fighter-pilot flying goggles to keep the dust out of their eyes. And to keep warm they wore huge ex-army leather overcoats with elbow-length leather gauntlets to staunch the rush of air that would otherwise have roared up their sleeves. As a concession to health and safety—as motorbikes didn't have indicators—riders would paint the outside edges of their right-hand gauntlets white so that car drivers behind you could easily see when you were turning right. But that's about as far as it went. Luckily, there weren't that many vehicles on the road.

There wasn't any need for heavy articulated vehicles as goods were mainly transported locally. Pick-up trucks were good enough for most jobs.

Cars were an enormous step up the social ladder. Relatively few people had them, and then it was largely well-off folk such as the doctor, bank manager and other local worthies. Mr Barker, a special constable who lived down our street, graduated from his motorbike and sidecar to a Trojan Bubble Car, which thrilled Mrs Barker who no longer had to dress up as though she were going to war. It was a three-wheeler with a single front door that opened to admit both passengers who sat side by side—an improvement on the Messerschmitt where the lid lifted off and the passenger had to sit behind the driver after the fashion of a small aircraft.

I was understandably very chuffed when dad brought home our first van—we were one of the first in our street to have a vehicle at all—

but it wasn't out of any sense of social-climbing. Dad's was the firm's van—necessary for carrying around water tanks and hot-water cylinders. The dark-green Austin A50 pick-up had a long bench seat so that Kath and I could sit in the middle with mum by the door and dad driving when we went out in it for the day, which we often did at weekends. We might go to the Dales or as far as the Lakes. We had a few favourite beauty spots we always liked to visit: the villages of Grassington, Bolton Abbey, Kettlewell, Appletreewick and Burnsall in particular.

A few years later the firm dad worked for replaced the larger van with a brown Austin Mini pick-up. Since there was now no room for Kath and me inside the cab we put a few cushions in the open back to make an improvised seat and bounced around over the rough country roads with just a plastic cover stretched over the top to protect us from dust and rain. It seems difficult to imagine today, when child-sized car seats and seat belts are compulsory. Added to the real possibility of bruising was the inhalation of toxic fumes from the exhaust, which the aerodynamics of the Mini van ensured were sucked into the back of the vehicle with astonishing efficiency.

Those were the great days of motoring. Not many people needed to use a car for getting to work in the fifties and early sixties; 'taking the car out for a run' was something you did for fun at weekends. Then you'd spend a few hours lovingly washing and leathering the bodywork and buffing-up the chrome, before putting it away in the garage again. Naturally the average cost-conscious car owner did most of his own maintenance and repairs. Cars had proper mechanical parts that you could take out, mend and put back—no fancy electronics or sealed units in those days—and in any case a new car came with a manual that told you how to do just about anything that might ever need doing. It was mostly the posher cars that were sent to a garage for attention. But even if cars were a bit short of fancy knobs and dials they'd usually have real leather seats and a walnut dashboard, so a car smelt like a car should, especially on a warm day when it had been standing in the sun—difficult to describe but once inhaled never forgotten.

Long car journeys were rare, but when you made one—perhaps to visit distant relatives or for your holidays—the journey was so exciting that there was none of the usual 'are we nearly there yet', and there was no plumbing your ears into your iPod to pass the time. We didn't have anything half so sophisticated. There was, very rarely, a primitive radio, but often the engine was so noisy that you couldn't hear it. Children who might have been a bit restless entertained themselves with *I-Spy* books, or they'd spot number plates— by looking the ending of the registration number up in the AA book, you could tell which county the car came from, and you soon learnt to identify those from your own area. UW and UM, WW and WX were West Riding favourites. Equally good sport was watching out for AA patrolmen on their motorbikes; in those days they always had to salute members, whom they recognized by the AA badge prominently mounted on the car. (Rumour had it that if an AA man failed to salute a member, it was a secret signal to let the driver know a police car was close by so they'd watch their speed and moderate any signs of flamboyance in their driving style.) Car-sick kids—and there was a lot of it about—passed the time anxiously sucking glucose sweets or barley sugar that came in special tins sold as 'travel sweets', trying to stave off the inevitable.

But the vehicles on the road at the time had romantic names that are a vintage-car lover's dream today. Not for us in the 1950s such banal and foreign-sounding names as Toyota Auris and Fiat Punto. Oh, no. We had Morris Oxfords and Austin Cambridges, Armstrong Siddeley Sapphires and Daimler Darts, Standard Eights and Ford Populars (the old sit-up-and-beg model, which only ever seemed to come in black). There were the ubiquitous Austin A30s and Morris Minors, and the 'half-timbered' Morris Traveller estate version.

I pleaded with dad to let me buy a black Ford Anglia in 1966 for £70, the entire contents of my bank account. He shook his head. 'It's not buying it,' he'd say, 'it's keeping it on the road. And anyway, the windscreen wipers don't work when you're going uphill.' He was right; they didn't. Dad coveted the majestic Rover 90, though at 5ft 8in he'd have had trouble seeing over the steering wheel. Me? I dreamed of a scarlet, raffish, MG TC sports car, like the doctor had, with a steering wheel that seemed to be made from polished ivory. And I looked enviously on the Rolls-Royce Silver Cloud owned by the local factory owner. It didn't roar past, it just purred.

The first BMC Minis started appearing around 1960. You could have the economy version with an 850cc engine but no heater for £497. All sorts of famous people had them: Peter Sellers, Ringo Starr, Twiggy and Marianne Faithfull, even

THE RISE OF MOTORWAYS

One evening in 1959, I was sitting in our living room at home watching the TV news, in black and white, when the first footage came through showing a brand new road that had just been opened. It was called the M1; our very first motorway.

It created one heck of a fuss. To think you could drive all the way from London to Leicester (well, almost) on the same road, without meeting a T junction, a roundabout or another motorist swerving across the road in front of you making a right turn. What's more there was no need to watch out for changing speed limits as you moved through towns and countryside; you could travel at a steady 70mph all the way if you wanted. In fact, you weren't allowed to drive slower than 40mph, and no pedestrians, push-bikes, horses or even learner-drivers were permitted, so you could just put your foot down and GO.

All of a sudden people were a lot keener to travel longer distances. It was all so much easier. A theory subsequently came to light that the reason for choosing this particular route for our very first motorway was so that MPs with a taste for fox-hunting at weekends could reach the Shires quickly and easily after leaving the House of Commons on Friday nights, and return to work just as easily on Monday mornings, but whether that's true I wouldn't like to say.

Princess Margaret and Lord Snowdon. The sixties also saw the Triumph Herald, the Ford Anglia with the famous inwardly sloping rear window, and the Ford Zodiac; you'd also see the occasional Dormobile—Uncle Bert had one, and when we went to see him and Auntie Edie, and my cousins Martin and Valerie, we'd all pile into it for a day out: four adults, four kids and two dogs. It was like a people-carrier with the addition of a few (very) basic camping features, but it seemed pretty special at the time, even though the heating was a bit hit and miss. I'd occasionally help him with his deliveries in winter, and he'd lift up the protective cowl that covered the engine transmission while we were driving along, the better to let the heat from the engine warm up the cab.

But, regardless of my dad's discouragement, I was not about to let the motoring revolution pass me by. The one thing any self-respecting young man urgently needed to do was learn to drive. It was, after all, your best chance of impressing girls, so you aimed to take your test as soon as possible after reaching the magic age of 17. I taught myself to drive from a book, seated at the piano in our living room. Well, at the time everyone had a piano while not many people had a car, so there was nothing else to practise on. It worked out very well. I sat on the piano stool with the instructions propped up on the music stand in front of me just above the keys, and used the soft and loud pedals as the accelerator and clutch. The gear lever— and this was the clever part—was a walking stick stood precariously in the hole in the bottom of a large upturned flowerpot stood on the floor to the left of the piano stool. The sound effects of engine revving or brakes screeching were all provided by me personally, until in moments of crisis when my 'vehicle' hurtled round fast corners, there'd be a flurry of sheet music all over the floor as the stool tipped over and the contents shot out, and I'd be told it was time to park the piano and go to bed. I passed my test at the first attempt, but it was a long time before I saw the footbrake as anything other than an optional extra.

Air travel

Air travel was still a very special event when I was growing up. Flying had started out in the 1920s and 1930s as a very genteel and upmarket means of travel for the seriously wealthy. These early travellers paid high prices for large comfy seats and first-class service throughout, but all the while in relatively small, cold, draughty, unpressurized aircraft with poor safety records. By the end of the Second World War aeroplanes had advanced enormously, but when passenger air travel was restored it was still first class only and at prices that most people couldn't afford. It was also fairly inconvenient; airports were small and scattered around the country at places like Croydon and Northolt, some distance from city centres. Our major airport for international flights was Hurn near Bournemouth, but that was soon to change.

Most international passengers came from the United States, where air travel was years ahead of us, and the American airlines wanted to be able to land passengers closer to London—the last thing their passengers wanted at the end of a long flight was a 100-mile road journey—so in

1950 an old RAF station called Heathrow was taken over for the purpose. Since it didn't have any facilities, canvas marquees and caravans were used as passenger lounges—early air travel still felt wonderfully intrepid. The rest is history; Heathrow now has five terminals, where passengers kill time waiting for their flights at luxury shops and restaurants, and a third runway is regularly on and off the cards.

Once the airlines realized mass-market travel might be a nice little earner, the aviation industry produced larger planes, packed them with smaller seats, removed all unnecessary 'frills' and introduced second-class tickets (known as 'tourist class' so as not to offend anyone) at much cheaper prices. And that's about how things stood at the time I came onto the scene, although we didn't fly off for holidays abroad at all during the time I lived at home with my parents. Mum was too nervous, so while Kath and I were growing up we only ever holidayed in Britain, where we could go by car or train. My first flight wasn't till I was twenty; we all went to Majorca, and I can't recall anything about it, so it must have been pretty uneventful.

Even when air travel had opened up to the masses, it was still quite a performance travelling by plane in the early days. The airline booking offices were in central London, and most passengers for Heathrow travelled up to London by train and from there took a taxi to the booking offices to check in—there the luggage was carefully weighed, and passengers were taken by bus to the airport. Once on board, you'd sit in your seat and because the cabins weren't pressurized, the air stewardesses handed out barley sugar just before take-off,

AIRLINE MEALS

It's easy to knock airline meals today, but in the early days of mass air travel there was a lot more to in-flight food and drinks than met the eye. Planes were unpressurized at the time, and some food and drinks reacted badly to the dry air and shortage of oxygen at high altitude; it also affected people's ability to taste things.

Mayonnaise and flying never mixed, so it was never served. Wines were a particular problem since a lot of them didn't take kindly to the constant vibration and changes of air pressure; champagne evidently came out best, followed by white wines and, of the reds, Bordeaux 'travelled' best by air. Once pressurized cabins came along all such restrictions ended. The only real casualty was the barley sugar.

with instructions to keep swallowing to equalize the pressure in your eardrums and counteract the uncomfortable popping sensation you'd feel otherwise. The barley-sugar routine also helped take your attention away from the nerves associated with take-off.

Since a lot of people were terrified of flying and were only being induced to overcome their fear in the first place by the relatively cheap price, anything that took your mind off it was seen as a good thing. That's why air hostesses always looked so stunning; they were chosen for their glamorous looks and good grooming, and then kitted out in fetching uniforms to distract at least the male passengers. (Rumour had it they weren't allowed to be married and were pensioned off from flight duties at quite an early age—a fair few of them, it has to be said, had already met and married well-heeled first-class passengers by then.) There wasn't much to do during your flight once you'd finished your barley sugar, except look forward to the second helping which was handed out just before landing.

As larger planes with bigger passenger-carrying capacity were introduced, long-haul trips, which had once taken several days with overnight stops and meals on the ground were replaced by more cost-effective services that meant spending longer in the air on airlines such as BOAC, British Overseas Aircraft Corporation, or BEA, British European Airways. Meals were taken in flight, distributed by air hostesses—again this helped to pass the time for passengers tightly strapped into small seats where they were packed elbow to elbow. They also had in-flight drinks and reclining seats so that passengers could catnap during long or overnight flights—airlines often handed out 'goodies' such as airline bags, overnight kits and soft floppy slippers to make long trips more comfortable, especially for those travelling first class.

The biggest innovation came in 1958 with the introduction of the first really successful jet airliner, the Boeing 707, which was capable of carrying 189 passengers. With a speed of 600mph it covered the distance between refuelling stops quickly, and instead of disembarking for a night at a hotel on the ground, passengers were put back on board after a short stop in the airport terminal. A trip that had previously taken over a week to complete in several legs could now be done in 60 hours of continuous

AIRLINERS

Planespotting took over from trainspotting as a pastime for small boys—and older ones, it has to be said—and could be done quite comfortably from the outdoor viewing points on the airport roof. (These were often seen in news broadcasts, packed with fainting and screaming female fans, any time The Beatles returned from trips to America.)

Small boys who'd once wanted to become train drivers now wanted to be airline pilots instead. It seemed like a very glamorous profession, with the huge salary, the mastery over large, highly technical chunks of macho machinery and the presence of so many good-looking unmarried stewardesses, but in practice there were few opportunities. Most airline captains were picked from the many ex-military pilots who came onto the job market when the armed forces were being trimmed back, and they came with lots of previous experience so taking them on was cheaper than training complete beginners from scratch. For many years hopeful schoolboys didn't get a look in.

travel with nothing more than brief refuelling breaks. This gave travellers a huge opportunity to broaden their horizons, but additional problems for the aircrew—much to the amusement of theatre audiences. The stage-play *Boeing-Boeing*, starring Brian Rix, was a farce showing the romantic problems of a philandering pilot when the introduction of Boeings altered the airline schedules, so that his various stewardess girlfriends narrowly missed meeting each other as they passed through his flat.

By the 1960s a lot of airlines were joining forces with travel firms to offer their own package holidays at below the cost of the return air fare alone, but small private companies were often able to undercut them. In this way two couples staying at the same hotel in the Bahamas might find that one had paid more than £200 and the other only £127 for exactly the same holiday. We started learning to shop around. But by the mid 1960s an annual summer holiday abroad had become a regular reality for most British people. Flights were faster, but in-flight entertainment was still way in the future—the best that might happen was that a few interested passengers, especially children, might be invited up to the cockpit to meet the captain and see the instruments. The kids back home would be green with envy.

Duty free

Few airline passengers today pass through an airport without availing themselves of the duty-free shop, but have you ever wondered how they came about?

Ever since the nineteenth century the customs and excise service had permitted travellers to enjoy, duty free, the unconsumed portion of tobacco, wine and perfumes that they took with them to use during a journey. Since the journey from major cities overseas—even Paris to London at one time—took a long time, in dirty and uncomfortable conditions, it was fair to assume that gents would want to refresh themselves and ladies to freshen up frequently during the journey, so the duty-free allowances were set at levels that allowed them to do so without stinting. And since people travelling by sea were allowed to buy goods duty free during the voyage, this concession was extended to airline passengers via duty-free shops. But because of the shorter journey time they were allowed to buy their 'travelling rations' before their journey started.

The very first duty-free shop in the world was at Shannon airport in Ireland, with others appearing in the 1950s. The original shops, however, were tiny—just a girl in a kiosk.

CHAPTER 4

THE WAY WE WERE ON THE FARM

Everyday country life seemed like a living, breathing version of *The Archers*—an everyday story of countryfolk when, as a lad, I cycled the streets and lanes all round Ilkley, or dad took us out for the day in his van. Apart from the open moors, the countryside was a checkerboard of small fields growing a wide range of different crops, divided up by hedges. There were still plenty of sizeable farming and sporting estates, and a large number of small family farms—an old man, his son and grandson could still make a living of sorts from as little as 20 acres. But they were real farms of the old school, not agri-businessmen. Farmers, large or small, didn't specialize in one main crop—they had a 'bit of everything'; they kept livestock and grew their own animal feed. A farmer bedded his beasts down on straw left behind when his corn crop was harvested, and it went back onto the fields as manure. Nothing was wasted.

Tractors had first begun to be a common sight in the countryside around the end of the Second World War, but in the 1950s they were still quite small and only pulled basic equipment, and a few of the smaller, more traditional-minded farmers still used horses. Up until the end of the first half of the twentieth century most crops were grown the traditional way, using very few chemicals (well, there weren't that many available, and small farmers couldn't afford them anyway) so the

DDT

It was at the beginning of the Second World War that the insecticidal properties of DDT were discovered, firstly as a way of reducing the incidence of malaria by controlling mosquitoes. It quickly became an all-purpose insecticide, often used indiscriminately to control all manner of insect pests. But by the 1960s it was found to build up to dangerous levels in body fat and its use was discontinued.

In 1962 the American biologist Rachel Carson highlighted the perils of persistent insecticides in her book Silent Spring, which sent shock-waves around the world. She blamed DDT for causing thinner eggshells in birds and thus having a disastrous effect on bird numbers in the countryside. Her call to arms resulted in the chemical being banned in the United States in 1972. It was not until 1984 that its use was banned in the UK.

countryside was full of birds and cornfields were full of wildflowers. Corn was cut in sheaves and straw was stacked in traditional haystacks, so the countryside *looked* traditional too.

A lot of agricultural jobs still had to be done by hand, so farming generated plenty of rural jobs. Country life flourished; small farmers usually sold their produce directly to local shops and some even ran their own milk rounds. The land was in good hands. Farmers were, and still are, guardians of the countryside. In the 1940s and 1950s that involved tending stiles, maintaining hedges and ditches, and caring for the soil; not just for their own good, but for other users of the countryside such as the hunt or for shooting parties, and most important of all, for the future generations of farming sons who were confidently expected to follow in their fathers' footsteps. It came as a great surprise when, only a few years later, youngsters preferred to go off to university, and go into high-flying, high-paying desk jobs where they didn't have to get up early in the mornings or get their hands dirty, and farms were worked by contractors using enormous pieces of machinery that needed all the hedgerows to be ripped out to create huge, open, prairie-style fields.

Life on the farm

Farms came in all sizes, so there was far more diversity than we find today, which all helped to give the countryside its character.

There were still plenty of large farming estates run by wealthy landowners who lived on the spot in 'the big house'. Estates like these had most likely been owned by the same wealthy family for many generations, and were run by the landowner with the help of a manager and a large permanent staff consisting of stockmen, tractor drivers and general farm workers. These were skilled people who worked long unsociable hours in all weathers, often in dirty, wet, uncomfortable and often dangerous conditions ('health and safety' hardly existed). They had little time off and few holidays since cows need milking twice daily, every day, and the harvest needed bringing in on time, regardless. But farming was a job men either loved or got out of, so they got on with it and thought how lucky they were to be out in the open air and not have to work in hot,

90

Farming was a family affair, with sons learning the ropes from their fathers.

noisy factories. At least, that's what they thought on bright spring and summer days! If the estate was also used for shooting there would be a gamekeeper and an underkeeper or two. Quite a few of the older farm workers and gamekeepers were ex-soldiers invalided out of the Great War, who'd been advised to work outdoors for the sake of their health. At busy times the estate would also hire in as many casual workers as it needed. (They weren't hard to find—the countryside was full of people who took on a variety of seasonal employment throughout the year, besides people who held down several part-time jobs.)

The permanent members of staff were housed in rent-free tied cottages on the estate. Even though wages were low there were quite a few perks for full-time farmhands, so they could live fairly comfortably by the standards of the time, even if cash was a bit short. They could collect firewood from the woods, they often had free milk—which they collected daily from the dairy in a milk can—maybe also free vegetables, eggs and a turkey at Christmas, all depending on what else the estate produced. Farmhands picked the blackberries and other wild fruit from the hedge-rows and the wild mushrooms that proliferated in the pastures (some of which were never ploughed up). They would learn, early on, which ones were poisonous and which were not. Today most wild fungi are left untouched by workers whose fungus identification skills are not on a par with their predecessors.

Staff on sporting estates fared even better; the staff might be given a few rabbits, pigeons and the occasional brace of pheasant. And most tied cottages had a garden large enough to keep a few hens and grow some veg, so workers were fairly self-sufficient. They had very little need for cash. Since their tied cottages were very basic there were no water or electricity bills to pay, so what money they earned was available to spend on a few Woodbines, a night at the village pub or those household necessities that you didn't make or grow for yourself. The only drawback to what might have seemed like an idyllic lifestyle was that everything was dependent on the job—if you got the sack, you lost *everything*—income, house and life-support system. No wonder the landowner and estate manager were treated with such huge respect; people couldn't afford to fall foul of them.

But there were also lots of small family farms, whose owners were still highly respected members of the local community who made a very good living, thanks to farm subsidies. This was a system of government payments that had been brought in during the War to make Britain as self-sufficient as possible, and then continued afterwards to make sure the country's food supplies were secure. Some small farms were run by tenants on land rented from the church or other large landowners, but the vast majority were small family-owned farms which had been handed down through generations, and worked almost entirely by the men of the family with the help of casual labour at busy times.

But it wasn't unusual at the time for farming families to have seven or eight children, so there was no shortage of free home-grown help. Children from the age of seven would be up and out before school milking the cows (which was sometimes still done by hand on small farms with only a few cows) or doing the milk round, and at harvest all hands were needed to gather the crops. It was quite normal for children of farming families to be kept away from school to help out at busy times—nobody batted an eye and even teachers took it for granted—after all, children of small family farmers were merely learning how to do what they'd be doing for the rest of their lives, so a 'formal education' was seen as something of an optional extra. Harvest-time was a big feature of rural life. Half the village would turn out to help, unasked, and in return for wages they'd get the odd few bales of straw or some corn for their own hens. The harvest festival, held at the local church when all was safely gathered in, really meant something to a generation that still depended on its farming roots. It was a big occasion. Even today in our village church, farmers who are not to be seen there at any other time of year will turn up for the harvest festival. It is their nod in the direction of the almighty—a way of expressing thanks, and relief, for another year of getting away with it.

The farming year

In the 1940s and 1950s the farming year followed a natural cycle that was repeated relentlessly every year. Fields were ploughed in winter or early spring, then shortly before sowing they were smoothed over with the harrow—like a gardener raking the soil, but on a bigger scale. During the growing season a certain amount of attention would be needed periodically before harvesting, which took place during summer and autumn. Each crop had its own particular foible; the great advantage of growing 'a bit of everything' was that routine jobs slotted into the sequence in turn, and the harvest was staggered so workers could move from one crop to another instead of having to tend the whole farm at once. Then in winter it was time to take care of maintenance work on farm buildings and equipment, and go 'hedging and ditching'. Ditches were cleared of any brambles and weeds and the silt would be dug out of the bottom so they'd channel rainwater away and help to drain the adjacent fields. The hedges alongside were trimmed well before the bird-nesting season. Quite a few were still being traditionally 'laid', which turned a hedgerow into a thick living fence of interwoven stems that kept livestock in and also made it a lot slower growing so it needed less attention. Even today you'll see hedge laying in progress, undertaken by farmers who value the skills of craftsmen and the benefits to wildlife—and sheltered crops—that result from their labours.

Towards the end of the winter or in early spring, fields had a visit from the muck-spreader, when manure from the farm livestock which had been piled up in the midden pit would be redistributed back onto the land. Farmers without tractors would spread muck using a horse-drawn cart and a device that half-tipped the stuff off into heaps. A good horse would know the job by heart and go to the next spot and stop ready for the next heap to be dropped off, without any instructions from the driver. When all the manure had been dropped off in heaps, they would be spread by hand with a fork, and the whole lot would be turned in when the ground was ploughed. Farmers tried to get their ploughing done before the end of winter, since the frost did a lot of the cultivation for them, breaking up large clods so there was less for the harrows to do before sowing in spring. A lot of traditional farmers bemoaned the passing of horses, since they reckoned the weight of a tractor would compress the ground so much that crops wouldn't grow as well—or possibly wouldn't grow at all. It's true that horses didn't compact the soil so badly; what's more, in wet conditions farmers could often plough with horses when a tractor would just have got bogged down. But farmers couldn't help being impressed by the work rate of tractors. What's more they started at the turn of a handle; a chap didn't need to get up *quite* so early each morning when there was no need to feed, muck out and harness up before starting work, followed by another long session in the stables at the end of work every evening.

Horse power v tractors

A team of two horses pulling a single furrow plough could cover an acre of ground in one day's work—in fact, that was the original definition of an acre. The ploughman who steered and guided the horses walked behind giving instructions by voice and using the long reins, and between them they'd have walked 18 miles going up and down rows as they ploughed their day's acre.

Even small tractors like the post-war Fordsons and 1950s' 'Little Grey Fergie' (as the T20 is still affectionately known by vintage tractor enthusiasts) could plough twice the depth of a horse-plough and cover roughly four times the area every day, even though they still pulled a single furrow plough. Larger more powerful tractors and many-furrowed ploughs now make it possible for one man and many thousands of pounds' worth of equipment to plough over 20 acres a day, and with headlights they can keep going late into the night.

Farm crops

In my youth you never saw yellow fields of oilseed rape or blue fields of flax in the countryside; it was all traditional crops like potatoes, wheat or barley, depending on whereabouts you lived, and a lot of farmland was taken up with pasture or crops for feeding to the livestock. Seen from a distance, all the different colours and textures of far-off farm crops helped to give the countryside its characteristic patchwork-quilt appearance; all very chocolate-boxy, and the stuff of childhood memories.

Sugar beet was an important crop in the flatlands of East Anglia. The big fat roots, like giant parsnips, were grown for processing into granulated sugar, as a cheaper alternative to importing sugar produced overseas from tropical sugar cane.

But in those days growing sugar beet was an extremely labour-intensive job. Shortly after the seedlings came up, they had to be thinned out to the correct spacing by teams of casual workers using hoes. A little later they had to be 'singled', since each sugar beet 'seed' was actually a cluster of several seeds which grew all together in a tight clump; if all the seedlings in the clump had been allowed to grow the plants would have been overcrowded, resulting in their roots being small and stunted, so each 'clump' had to be thinned out to leave just the strongest seedling. Since there was no miracle product or even a piece of machinery that could do the job, it had to be done by hand— by women and children, using their fingers. Later in the season more teams of workers would go through the beet fields again, hoeing out all the weeds that came up; they'd have to tackle each field twice before the crop was finally harvested. Even when herbicides came in they were so expensive that a lot of small farmers found it more cost-effective to continue paying casual labour to hoe the fields by hand.

Years later seed firms were able to supply sugar beet seed that didn't come up in clumps, but it wasn't 100 per cent single seeds, so even in my twenties it was still quite common in East Anglia to see an old chap wrapped in sacking against the biting cold and rain, working out on his own in the middle of a huge field with a hoe. A whole field would take days to do; it must have been miserable work. But the misery didn't end there. Sugar beet was the last crop to be harvested because the roots were almost indestructible—they could safely be left in the ground till after Christmas if need be, to stagger the year's farm work. 'Lifting' as it was called went on between October and January, any time the ground wasn't too boggy for tractors and trailers to work. The beets were lifted out of the ground mechanically, but the tops had to be chopped off by hand They were collected up and fed to bullocks, and the 'bits and pieces' left in the fields were an important food source for huge flocks of wild geese which visited East Anglia every winter. Meanwhile the sugar beet roots were sent off to the processing factories for the sugar to be extracted, and the pulp left over afterwards was used to feed cattle. Once again, nothing was wasted.

Cereal crops, known collectively as 'corn', were either wheat, barley or oats (though oats were normally only grown in Scotland and the North of England). They were all sown in spring in those days, and when the rows of grassy shoots first came through, fields of cereal crops looked like giant

98

lawns for a few weeks till the stalks grew tall and started rippling in the breeze. Once the immature green heads of corn formed it would be time for gangs to go through the fields pulling out wild oats. These were one of the worst weeds of cereal crops, and if left their seeds would get mixed with the 'proper' crop which reduced its value, so they had to come out. Wild oats were easy to tell from wheat or barley, since they grew two feet taller with big, loose, shaggy seedheads. 'Rogueing' as weeding-out wild oats was known, had to be done by hand. The job was a useful little earner for children, unskilled youths and women as it was relatively light work compared to a lot of casual farm jobs. (Modern weedkillers have put paid to wild oats today, so modern crops never need rogueing.)

But apart from this cereal crops weren't a lot of work till harvest time, which started in summer. Barley was ready to cut in late July and early August, then in late August or early September the workers would move on to the wheat. The combine harvester would work its way round the edges of the fields first, moving slowly into the centre. As the machine moved onto the final patch of corn in the middle of the field, you'd see dozens of rabbits that had taken cover in the remaining crop suddenly dash for the safety of the hedgerows, and that's the moment the farmhands would pot a few with the shotguns they'd brought with them especially. (Some things never change!)

Large bundles of cornstalks were tied up in sheaves which were then 'stooked'—stood on end in groups of eight in a wigwam shape to finish drying out. They'd be left for a week or so, when farmers hoped for dry, breezy weather, before being stacked under a temporary thatched roof waiting for the arrival of the threshing machine sometime during the autumn or winter, which separated the grain from the strawy stalks. The straw would be baled then stacked and used for bedding livestock in winter. (Corn crops always had long stems in those days, so there was always plenty of straw to go round.) Meanwhile the grains of cereal went off to a factory for processing. Wheat was mostly milled to make flour, but some—the poorer quality stuff— went for animal or chicken feed. Barley was grown for malting to make beer but only the best was good enough and the rest went into animal feed, mostly for pigs. As for oats, the best went for porridge oats and the rest again ended up as animal feed.

After the harvest, the fields were left untouched until late winter or early spring. Farmers would turn their sheep out onto stubblefields to forage for any spilt grain left on the ground, but winter stubblefields also attracted hordes of songbirds whose numbers declined hugely after farmers began to plough the land straight after the harvest in order to put in autumn-sown wheat. And because fields of corn were harvested relatively late, skylarks had time to nest and raise their young before the combines came round, so there were lots more birds around farmland than you see now. Today a single giant combine harvester cuts and threshes corn crops in a single pass, disgorging clean grains straight into a trailer, then within a short time of harvest another huge tractor comes round ploughing or—more frequently nowadays with the increased use of shallow tillage—merely chopping the stubble in with large harrows, before the next crop is sown. Fields are rarely left idle for long, so it's no wonder our traditional countryside songbirds are having a tough time surviving.

Hay was another crop that was widely grown by small farmers to feed their livestock in the winter. Well, when you grew your own using family labour, it was virtually free. In the 1950s the countryside still had plenty of permanent hayfields that had never been ploughed up, so the fields were packed with a wide range of different grasses and wildflowers, and this mixture produced first-rate hay. (Go to Upper Teesdale today and you'll see wildflower meadows that you thought only existed in Switzerland.) The crop would be cut once a year, in summer, and left in the field to finish drying in the sun before being baled and stored in the barn for winter. After the hay had been cleared away the farmer would turn his cows out on the field to graze on the regrowth, and then each winter the field would be given a dressing of muck (as manure was affectionately known) to encourage strong new growth next season. No chemicals or fertilizers were used at all.

Because this type of hayfield was left undisturbed and grown by traditional methods, not only did wildflowers thrive but farmland birds such as corncrakes did too. But that wasn't the only way farmers grew hay crops. Sometimes they'd undersow a crop of corn with a mixture of clovers and grasses, which grew slowly, so that when the corn was cut the hay could grow up, and this would be left for maybe five years, being cut once or twice each year, before being ploughed in so the field could be resown with corn again. But it was still very natural and allowed a lot of wildlife to flourish,

101

HOPS

I remember the litany from my school days when I learnt that Kent was famous for 'Hops, wheat, sugar beet.' Nowadays the acreage of hops grown in the UK is much reduced. In the part of Hampshire where I now live there were still 580 acres in 1960, but most of them disappeared 10 or 20 years ago as cheaper imports meant the crop was no longer worth cultivating. But traditionally hops were widely grown in these parts, and the 'bines'— the rough, twisting stems along with their clustered, pouch-like fruits—were sold at farm gates for decorating pubs and kitchens in country houses. A vital part of the brewing industry, they would be trained up great frameworks of poles and wires and harvested not only by the locals but by gypsies and travellers keen to make a bit of extra money.

The artist Alfred Munnings came to Hampshire from his home in East Anglia regularly between the 1930s and 1950s to paint them, their horses and their colourful caravans.

besides contributing to a traditional-looking countryside.

Peas and field beans were two other traditional crops that farmers grew in quantity. They were easily recognized since they looked exactly like peas and broad beans that grow in gardens, but instead of being picked to use fresh for the pot, the pods were left to mature and turn yellow on the plants.

When the seeds inside had dried out and turned bullet-hard, they were harvested and the dry peas or beans would be mixed with other seeds such as tares, oats or barley and used to make animal feeds. You still sometimes see fields of peas or beans grown today, though perhaps not so frequently.

Vegetables for human consumption were grown on a large scale in some places where the soil was suitable. Carrots were an important crop for farmers in the fens of East Anglia as the rich, fertile, silty, stone-free soil grew long carrots that were perfectly straight, so they made good prices when they were harvested in October. Bedfordshire was known for its brassicas, especially Savoy cabbages and sprouts, which were all picked by hand throughout the winter using huge gangs of casual workers who were very solidly dressed against the cold and wet. By the end of winter the smell of rotting cabbage hung in the air something chronic; seasoned travellers often claimed they could tell when they were in Bedfordshire by the characteristic aroma. And Cheshire was known for its new potatoes, which needed a lot of hand-work—especially for weeding and digging up—before being sold in July. Farmers near west-coast ports brought over Irish labourers specially. The same gangs often came back for years on end. Nowadays you'll still see fields of vegetables, but in these weight-watching days you'll also see huge acreages of lettuce in many parts of the country, greenhouses packed with tomatoes along the south coast and plastic tunnels full of strawberries around the Evesham area. And instead of locals cutting veg and picking fruit you're most likely to find eastern Europeans at work in the fields.

'**Fodder crops**' was the name given to things that were grown especially for feeding to livestock, mainly cattle, and they included kale, turnips, swedes and mangel-wurzels (which are large, coarse roots rather like a cross between a sugar beet and a swede). This extra food would be stored until needed and used in winter when there wasn't much grazing. And at shooting estates a lot of the fields would have wide bands of kale sown round the edges to provide winter feed and cover for game birds. Nowadays you'll still see cover for game birds (even pampas grass is used) since the price of a day's shooting has shot up, but livestock are largely fed on concentrated food in pellet form out of a sack.

Livestock

Factory farming was unheard of; most animals lived a reasonably natural life outside, except perhaps at night or when brought inside for calving or lambing. Most small farmers aimed to keep a big range of livestock to keep local butchers supplied. A lot of the livestock were not the fast-fattening hybrids we see today, but traditional old-fashioned kinds that suited non-intensive production methods and took time to rear—the kinds that today we'd call rare breeds.

The favourite farmyard hens were dual-purpose birds, kept for both egg-laying and meat. The ones most farmers favoured were the ever-popular Rhode Island Red, which laid brown eggs, but there were also a lot of Buff Orpingtons—fluffy ginger birds that produce big brown eggs; for pure white eggs people kept Light Sussex, which were white with black 'collars and cuffs'. After a couple of years, when a hen's laying days were done, it would end up in the pot as a 'boiling hen'. Stewed slowly for several hours with a carrot, an onion and perhaps a leek, it was very tasty—far more so than a modern roasting chicken which only lives for about six weeks and spends its entire life in a cage. The big problem for 1950s farmers was trying to keep hens laying right through the winter, when low-light conditions meant that instead of laying an egg a day they'd go 'off lay' for several weeks. That's when they started bringing hens into deep-litter sheds and keeping electric lights on, to make them think it was summer. But it was all still very non-intensive compared to what happens today.

Cattle were kept in small herds, mainly for milk production. Small farmers only had about 15 cows or so; 30 would have been thought of as a big herd at the time. But even farmers who didn't keep cattle for profit usually kept a house cow to provide milk for their own family—when farmers had eight children, they could easily get through a gallon or two of fresh milk every day. The favourite breeds were the black and white Friesians or Shorthorns. The latter were popular because they were a dual-purpose breed, which meant at the end of their working life they'd still provide a carcase that could be sold as meat or shared out round the family. It would be quite tough because the cow would be getting on a bit by then, but it was still good enough for stews and casseroles if it was cooked slowly for a long time. Farming families were known for enjoying good, hearty, traditional home cooking, and lots of it.

Milking took up a good deal of time, and it had to be done twice a day, all year round. A few small farms still milked their cows by hand, but small electric-powered milking parlours were coming into regular use. Once out of the cow, the milk went to an outbuilding known as 'the dairy'—every farm had one—where it was cooled before it was put into churns that were put out at the gate for collection once a day by a contractor who took it to a big collection centre for pasteurizing and bottling. Those who relied on their milk sales for part of their profit had a neat little trick up their sleeve. Friesians and Shorthorns were both good, reliable, heavy-yielding breeds but their milk was a bit low in butterfat, and since housewives liked their gold top, cream and butter in those pre-healthy-eating days, a lot of farmers would also keep a few Jersey cows. By mixing the extra-rich milk from these in with the rest of the farm's output they'd raise the butterfat content so they'd be paid a bit more for the whole batch. Besides the usual gold or silver top you could also buy sterilized milk in those days—it came in different-shaped bottles and had a slightly 'funny' taste, which a lot of people didn't like, because it had been heated to a higher temperature than the normal pasteurization process. It was all to do with tuberculosis—there had been a lot of it about in the human population for many years, and it was difficult to treat at the time. TB testing for cattle came in during the 1950s, and you'd know if you'd bought milk from TB-tested herds because it said so on the bottle. It was something housewives looked for. But a lot of small farmers' families

106

drank untreated milk virtually straight from the cow.

Pigs were mostly Large Whites, though a few traditional farmers in some counties still kept the old black-and-white Saddlebacks, so-called because of the white 'saddle' pattern across the middle of their black backs. Pigs were fed very economically on swill. When the farmer cleaned his dairy down and washed his milk churns out, a weakly diluted solution of milk would be *swilled* out (hence the name)—and that was mixed with ground-up wheat and poured into a trough for the pigs. Some farmers also collected edible waste from

Pigs were rather like giant dustbins,
eating every scrap the farmer could find.

schools, restaurants and hospital kitchens or even private houses daily in specially covered bins, rather like giant dustbins, and mixed that in as well after boiling it well first to kill off any germs. We had a man come down our street every day when I was a lad, and he tipped our small bins of potato peelings and the like that had been put out for him into half a dozen metal dustbins he towed behind his van in a trailer. We never thought to call it recycling; he was just 'the pig man'.

The end result of this rich and varied diet was a very fat pig, producing joints with thick layers of fat that yielded lovely dripping. And they were *happy* pigs. They were kept out of doors, in fields where they were free to rootle around, lie down in muddy puddles and frolic. Each sow would be given a little hut with lots of straw for bedding, where she'd have her litter of piglets and be able to bring them up naturally. (These days you can still find pigs produced this way—travel down the A303 in Wiltshire to see a fair few of them—and the meat from those animals is high quality and in

Boulton and Paul started out as an ironmongers in Norwich, although they manufactured aircraft during the War.

108

big demand by pork lovers concerned about animal welfare.) At appropriate moments the boar would be sent for, and the cycle would start up again. A fair-sized farmer owning perhaps a dozen or 15 sows would keep his own boar; several small farmers might club together and share a boar between them or else they'd 'borrow' the services of someone else's in return for a few piglets from the resulting litter. Country children never needed to be taught the facts of life; they'd see what went on for themselves from their bikes or the bus as they passed through the fields on their way to school.

Sheep were kept for meat because there was very little demand for wool. Everyone in the 1950s and 1960s wanted the latest new synthetic fibres, which were more fashionable, for fabrics and clothing. But there were still plenty of sheep around. The various breeds had evolved over centuries to meet local conditions, so you'd see different kinds all round the country. In hilly areas the local sheep had to be exceptionally hardy to equip them for outdoor life in very rugged conditions. Herdwicks, which it's claimed were first brought over by the Vikings, were found right across the northern part of the country from the Lake District into Northumberland. They look a bit piebald; many of them have dark brownish fleeces and white heads, others are white with black heads and some are all off-white. They are well known for their habit of 'hefting': they learn their own territories on unfenced hills and dales and pass this knowledge onto their lambs, so they don't wander off. Wensleydale sheep are big, tall, long-legged sheep with a long shaggy fleece that looks

COTTAGE INDUSTRIES

Livestock, such as ducks, geese and guinea fowl, were a good little earner for some small farmers because they ran round the yard and largely looked after themselves. They'd often be taken charge of by the farmer's wife and sold at the market to make some welcome cash for Christmas, though a fair few would end up as Sunday lunches at the farmhouse.

Even smallholders and country cottagers kept a few hens and sold their surplus eggs at the garden gate for 'pin money'. Most of them also kept a pig, fed on all the scraps from the kitchen and garden. To them it was just like a compost heap, but better because besides yielding high-quality manure it had a useful bonus at the end of the year in the form of bacon and hams. When you also kept a few hens and a well-stocked veg patch you could live very well for a small outlay, especially if you had a free source of grain and straw in return for lending a hand at harvest time.

It all helped to make ends meet—and as times become harder today, more and more people, even in towns, are again starting to keep a couple of hens as pets that pay their keep, in smart coops on the garden lawn, while the hottest gardening trend is now the cultivation of fruit and veg. Funny how, if you wait long enough, things come round again . . .

like dreadlocks—a mass of enormous ringlets—but it's very warm and waterproof and makes robust sweaters that really keep out the cold, even if they are a tad itchy.

The sheep I saw all over the moors above Ilkley—and which would occasionally find their way down into town to the consternation of motorists—were Swaledales, which are a hardy Yorkshire breed with off-white bodies and black heads and faces with just a butterfly of white at the ends of their noses. They are still very popular with sheep farmers in the area today. Hill sheep like these would be turned out on rough upland pastures spring and summer, then brought back down to the valleys in winter and kept in a field closer to farm buildings, where they might be given some hay to eke out the grass, especially in a wild winter when the ground might be covered by snow for weeks on end; but otherwise they were mostly left to manage on their own. They'd even have their lambs outside without assistance, though the shepherd would look them over occasionally, just in case of emergencies.

In lowland Britain, farmers kept sheep breeds such as the Suffolk, Leicester, Dorset and Norfolk. Sheep like these were handy for small mixed farms since they could be moved onto fields after arable crops had been harvested to take advantage of any edible oddments that were left behind which would otherwise go to waste. The lowland 'sheep year' began in spring with lambing; a shepherd would bring in imminent ewes and keep them under supervision in an outbuilding divided into 'booths' by straw bales, or in some places they lambed in the fields just with a bit of tarpaulin over one area as a cover. Any orphan lambs were adopted by sheep

111

that had lost their own lambs—the dead lamb would be skinned and the coat used to cover the impostor so the mother accepted it, and after a few days she'd bring it up as her own. But it still often fell to a farmer's wife to hand-rear orphan lambs that were left on the shelf so to speak; it took time and a warm farmhouse kitchen with an Aga-style range and a baby's bottle for feeding.

Early in summer sheep had to be sheared, even if, as often happened, the wool was just thrown away. It was all to do with animal welfare—in summer sheep would suffer from the heat unless their natural woolly overcoats were trimmed off. Sheep also had to be dipped every year to stop blowflies laying eggs, especially round the mucky rear end of the animals; left alone, the eggs would hatch out into maggots that burrowed into the skin and caused all sorts of unpleasant problems. But dipping wasn't much fun, for sheep or shepherds. First the sheep had to be rounded up into pens, then one by one run through a deep tank of pesticide solution sunk into the ground; as each sheep fell in it had to be pushed right under—head and all—with a crook. Everyone was glad when the job was over for the year.

Horses—that is heavy horses, usually shires—were the original tractors, with the big advantage that they produced their own free replacements and, with luck, they might also yield a few spares that could be sold at a profit. Although most farmers had changed over to tractors by the time I was growing up, a few small farmers still kept horses, if not for the big jobs like ploughing then at least for pulling carts or muck spreaders; they could do the job better than tractors in difficult conditions. They were also useful for ploughing confined spaces, awkward corners and the headlands of small fields where even small tractors couldn't easily work, and well into the 1960s East Malling Research Station in Kent still used horses to cultivate the narrow strips of ground between rows of fruit trees where there wasn't enough room for tractors to go.

While there were still horses used on farms, a lot of space had to be reserved for growing the crops used for feeding them. Horses needed large daily meals of hay and oats to enable them to do regular heavy work, since they clearly couldn't spend all day grazing on grass when they were out working. Farmers also saved the loose husks and grains known as 'chaff' that fell out of the threshing machine at harvest time; they added this to rolled oats, chopped hay, bran and treacle to make a muesli-like mixture known in some areas as 'chop', which horses loved. When it came to accommodation they'd need a field and a stable, plus a cart shed to store their harnesses and other equipment. But what a sight they were! They contributed to the traditional look of the British countryside, and when you saw a team of horses working—pulling farm carts or a plough—the hairs on the back of your neck would stand on end. They still do, if you see them in action at agricultural shows or in ploughing matches at countryside fairs.

CHAPTER 5

THE WAY WE WERE AT SCHOOL

School was much more than a place you went to learn the three Rs—reading, writing and 'rithmetic. You met old friends, made new ones, gained valuable life skills, played games, learned crafts and acquired a sense of responsibility—even if it was just by being milk monitor. We weren't put under enormous pressure to pass exams at all costs, at least not in primary school, as often happens today. Our teachers knew that not all children were natural eggheads, and university was something only a small proportion of the brainiest pupils with well-heeled parents would go on to. A lot of us were more practically minded and would end up working with our hands in one way or another. Which was probably just as well since in the 1950s there were only so many jobs for doctors, lawyers and civil servants, but the country needed lots of manual workers to run the factories, steelworks and coal mines that created wealth, not to mention building workers to rebuild and repair housing that had been damaged during the War.

School days were mostly quite good fun, but as you moved on up through the school system you became well aware that as soon as you'd finished your full-time education, you'd be expected to start earning your own living straight away, pay your mother for your keep, and eventually—as a chap—to provide a home and support a wife and family. The best years of your life? Well, schooldays

114

may have been for some, but a lot of us saw it as something you had to get out of the way before getting stuck in to what you really wanted to be doing.

The school

My first proper school was New County Infants School where I went at the age of five. I rather enjoyed it. We were taught to read with *Janet and John* books, we learnt our numbers, had our dinner in the school hall (which is what happened at most infant schools at the time) and generally larked about, singing and painting and being told stories. After three years, aged eight, I was moved on to Ilkley All Saints Junior School, which was a rather more serious affair in a sooty stone-built Victorian schoolhouse. It wasn't unusual. School buildings were a tad primitive at the time. To cope with the post-war baby boom some had expanded into 'temporary' prefab huts (which were still 'temporary' 20 years later), but a lot of Victorian school buildings were still in use. Some of them still had separate entrances for 'boys' and 'girls' even though everyone used the same door by now, and the classrooms still had the original fittings. There were ancient desks—the old double sort which sat two pupils side by side, with china inkwells—lined up in rows. At the front of the class the teacher used a blackboard (the famous talk and chalk teaching method); we copied out lessons into exercise books with pencils until we were old enough to use fountain pens (I *never* used a Biro at school); there were no visual aids or TVs, and computers hadn't been thought of.

Some classes were enormous by today's standards. It wasn't unusual for a teacher to have charge of 45 or 50 children, but in those days we were all quite well behaved, apart from one or two boys in each class, but a healthy dose of humiliation by the teacher was usually effective in silencing them. I suppose it helped not having E numbers in the food to make us hyperactive, but I think it was mostly down to upbringing. Good manners were instilled in us from an early age, so by the time we started school we'd already learnt to do as we were told without question, and we automatically respected authority figures like teachers and especially the headmaster or headmistress. You could argue that we were a bunch of unquestioning goody-goodies, but the truth was that most of us just wanted a quiet life!

We all walked or cycled to school, often lugging huge satchels full of heavy books, so we had usually worked off the worst of our energy before we sat down in class. A few far-distant kids caught the bus, and very few parents used a car—there was no 'school run'. It wasn't something parents did, and in any case, if you'd arrived by car the other kids would have thought you were spoiled and 'soft'. Mothers would walk to school with the very smallest kids, but even that stopped as soon as you were big enough to go on your own—it was taken for granted that you'd be perfectly safe. Was it that there were fewer dangers for children in those days, or just that we didn't become paranoid by hearing about them on every single news bulletin?

State education in the 1950s meant that both primary and secondary (and some grammar) schools were mixed. Most private schools were

*Me aged 11, and Kath aged 6, in our
school photo.*

single sex so that fee-paying parents could be
assured that teenagers would concentrate on their
work and not waste their time trying to impress
the opposite sex. In secondary education everyone
wore full school uniform, and that included berets
for girls and caps for boys, all with the school badge
sewn on the front. The idea was that when everyone
dressed exactly the same you couldn't tell the rich
kids apart from the poor ones, so there'd be no
bullying, and no showing off because jewellery
and fashion items weren't allowed. Mothers quite
liked school uniforms, despite the initial expense,
because you wouldn't wear out your everyday
clothes and they'd last longer. Dressing identically
also meant that you'd never have risked bunking
off school or misbehaving on your way home—any
passing grown-up could tell straight away from your

SCHOOL MILK

You'd have to be a child of pre-Thatcher Britain to remember school milk. We each had a third of a pint, daily, for free. It dated back to the days when a lot of children were undernourished and suffered from rickets, so giving out free milk at school had once helped poor families a lot, but by my day it had become something of a mixed blessing. Lots of us hated school milk. In hot weather it would sometimes be warm or even start to taste a tad sour, while in cold winters it might be freezing. If left outside too long the silver cap would have been pushed off by a long, white sausage of frozen milk. That meant we had to stand the bottles on radiators to warm them up, which yet again made the contents taste sour.

In any case school milk always had a rather unappetizing, sad, greyish colour— even the cream on top. But there was no 'take it or leave it'; drinking your milk was compulsory. You took your cardboard straw from the special box and sucked away until it was finished. A lot of milk-haters went to enormous lengths to dispose of their daily dose, from pouring it into the inkwells or feeding it to the school cat to watering it onto the pot plants (from which a faint scent of sour milk could be detected in summer). After Mrs Thatcher 'Milk Snatcher' stopped school milk, the third-of-a-pint-sized milk bottles have largely vanished. And, I'd suggest, a lot of school kids were mighty relieved.

uniform which school you went to and report bad behaviour to the head, which meant a little mention at assembly the following morning. Or worse.

Discipline was strict. There was no shouting in the corridors when moving from one class to another, nor after the bell which signified the end of break. There was no talking in class, or indeed at any other time when school rules decreed you should stay silent. Pupils stood up when a teacher came into the room and didn't leave until formally dismissed at the end of the lesson. Any lapses in good discipline were dealt with straight away. If you were lucky you might be let off with a verbal ticking off. If you were told off in the playground the teacher might confiscate something you'd brought from home such as a skipping rope or roller skates.

But the biggest deterrent was corporal punishment. Quite minor offences such as talking in class or doodling in your exercise book might be dealt with by a smack on the hand or a crack over the knuckles with a ruler. One of my teachers at junior school always twisted the curl of hair on the nape of my neck, which really hurt. Some schoolmasters were good shots with the hard blackboard rubber, which was often deployed if he spotted a child who wasn't paying attention or who was staring at something more interesting going on outside the window. More severe misdemeanours usually meant an appointment with the head for what might be a serious talking to or 'six of the best' with the cane on the bum or the palms of the hands. Looking back people say 'it never did me any harm', but it jolly well hurt at the time. And yet, it wasn't so much the pain that did the trick, but the humiliation.

Pupils were taught to act responsibly from quite an early age. Some of those who were considered reliable enough to take on day-to-day school chores were made monitors, with special duties. It was quite a feather in your cap to be chosen, though you'd have to take some stick from those who had not been singled out for such privileges. The blackboard monitor was responsible for cleaning the blackboard and beating the dusters that teachers used during lessons. They'd also have to put out new sticks of chalk when necessary, and visit the stationery cupboard to top up supplies periodically. (This in itself was quite a privilege because the cupboard was kept locked and you had to be accompanied by the school secretary who kept the key.)

Science monitors donned laboratory overalls to keep their school uniforms clean while they watered the plants on the biology lab windowsill or fed ants' eggs to the goldfish in the school aquarium. At schools that still had inkwells—and lots did— ink monitors were needed (one for each class) to top up the china receptacles set into the special hole provided in each desk, using a great enamel jug from the supply in the stationery cupboard. But the toughest job of all was milk monitor. The crates of milk were delivered to the school gates first thing in the morning and left standing outside until the mid-morning break, when a pair of milk monitors from each class would collect their crate— one holding each end since a full milk-crate was extremely heavy—and bring it back to distribute the contents, and make sure their classmates each drank their bottleful. It was a great responsibility.

The school day

The school day ran like clockwork according to a pre-determined timetable, with the start and finish of each lesson announced by bells. Strict punctuality was the absolute rule. The day always started with assembly, when the whole school 'assembled' in the main hall for a short act of worship—a hymn and a few prayers, followed by school notices. Then we'd file out to start class.

Infants stayed in the same classroom all day doing crafts such as making plasticene models, painting or cutting up bits of coloured paper. Christmas was a godsend for the teachers because they could get everyone making paper chains to decorate the classroom. Infants were also introduced to music, largely by singing, and enthusiastically bashing triangles, tambourines and cymbals, and clacking pairs of wooden clappers (castanets was far too foreign a word to use) in what passed for a percussion band. They would also do 'music and movement' under the guidance of a bright and breezy lady on the radio, who'd tell them to pretend they were flowers or something equally creative. But, most important, infants learnt to read, which paved the way for the most popular source of home entertainment—books. Well, nobody had TV, video or anything of the sort to pass the long evenings at home, so if you couldn't read you were going to have to listen to the wireless with your parents or be jolly bored.

Reading was taught using the traditional method that involved learning the alphabet, so we knew the sound of individual letters, and then joining them up to make words, which were helpfully shown as pictures to give you a clue. C-A-T cat, D-O-G dog, and that sort of thing. We learnt to write in much the same way, by copying out the letters individually and putting them together to make words, rather like reading but in reverse. And at this stage it was quite enough to know your capital letters and your little letters; joined-up writing wasn't expected until junior school. It must all sound so primitive to modern teachers, but we did all learn to read and write, and we knew our numbers, before going on to junior school.

By junior school, the pace was hotting up. Children had the same teacher who took all their lessons in every subject, for a year, before moving up a class. Lessons started to branch out into more specialist subjects. We did more spelling, English and arithmetic. Multiplication tables were learnt by rote; anyone visiting a primary school would have heard whole classrooms of kids chanting their 'times tables' in synch, and classroom walls were decorated with charts on which the teacher stuck stars to show which pupils had mastered which tables—we all aimed to score a full house. We did a bit more to develop our musical appreciation by singing and started to soak up some of the classics via records played on an ancient wind-up gramophone. We were introduced gently to subjects we'd start to study more seriously at senior school; we did a bit of scripture and learnt about prehistoric man—it sounded like lots of fun, living in caves or making huts of mud and branches, dressing in animal skins and bashing stones to make your own flint axes and knives. And we'd spend some time doing stuff I was very interested in—pressing flowers, growing pot plants from pips

*Secondary school was a more formal
affair. Where you went depended on the
results of your 11-plus examination.*

and rooting willows in jars of water, or germinating
broad beans in jars with damp blotting paper to
watch the roots grow.

But the emphasis on serious learning grew as
we moved up a class each year, so that at the age
of 11 the sheep would be sorted from the goats
by the obstacle that was the 11-plus exam. It was
a simple way of determining which senior school
you went on to; the brainy kids passed and went on
to the grammar school, and the rest of us went to
secondary school. I never saw it as a failure, just a
sort of natural selection process that made sure that
practically minded kids like me weren't lumbered
with six years of serious academic studies that we'd
never get to grips with and which would be no use
to us in later life. Well, how was I to know how
things would turn out?

At senior school, the day started with a longer
version of assembly that might include a short
bible reading by one of the senior pupils, with
perhaps the music teacher playing you in and out
of the hall on the battered upright piano. Then

123

SCHOOL EVENTS

Schools arranged all sorts of regular activities to which parents and any other family members who felt like turning out were invited.

There was the annual summer sports day, where you went in for races. This was back in the days when schools still encouraged pupils to be competitive, regarding it as an indicator of the life to come. Besides the usual running, long-jump and high-jump, there were more frivolous events. There'd always be an egg-and-spoon race where participants ran while balancing a whole, raw, real egg in a dessert spoon—the winner was the fastest over the finishing line with his or her egg still in place, and no glue was allowed. Get it wrong and you really did end up with egg on your face.

The three-legged race was run in pairs, with the inner legs of both participants tied firmly together so they hobbled rather than ran. It was all down to the timing—you needed to practise with your partner first to be in with any sort of chance. And in the sack race each participant stood inside a sack, which they held up at waist height, and then jumped inside it to the finishing line—naturally most of the entrants fell over and made complete idiots of themselves, which we all found hilarious. But most entertaining of all was the parents' race, where beefy great blokes battled it out with skinny clerkish-looking types, and a range of red-faced mothers (most of whom you never saw so much as break into a trot in normal circumstances) puffed and panted their way to the finishing line.

Bring-and-buy sales were organized each summer to raise funds. Nowadays we'd probably call them 'fêtes' which sounds a lot posher. Parents and teachers manned stalls selling jumble, cakes and home-made jams, second-hand books, outgrown school uniforms or surplus fruit and veg from their allotments, but the stall that always interested me most was the one packed with plants. It's always struck me as a brilliant way to recycle surplus cuttings and seedlings, by potting them up and passing them on, and for buyers there were real bargains to be had for sixpence or so. One of my teachers, Mr Rhodes, was a keen gardener who brought his home-grown cacti to the school sales where he'd sell them and pass on cultivation hints. I soon had a fair collection on my bedroom windowsill at home.

you'd return to your own classroom to collect up the right books before moving on to different classrooms for all your various lessons—maths, English and RE (religious education) in hour-long chunks throughout the day, according to where that particular teacher was based. By now we had a different one for each subject.

We were introduced to specialist subjects that we hadn't studied before such as French, history and geography. And in science lessons we experimented in the school laboratories with gas taps, Bunsen burners, bottles of various acids and heating things up in test tubes. Oh, it made you feel terribly important. And we stepped up the pace in subjects like music, art and drama, which we'd only done for fun before. Latin was a compulsory subject in most grammar schools in those days, even though most pupils wondered why they needed to learn a language that nobody spoke any more. At least French would come in handy on holiday. In the secondary school, woodwork and rural studies— the only two subjects I was any good at (apart from art)—were reserved for the B, C and D streams; we were graded according to our perceived intelligence. I suppose I should have been grateful I was in the A stream, but it did mean that I could only look into those classrooms with a wistful sigh.

At the age of 11 you were expected to organize yourself, keep tabs on your own personal timetable of lessons and make sure you had everything you needed for them. Woe betide anyone who didn't take the right books with them for the morning's lessons or who forgot to bring the right gym or football kit from home. Or who didn't hand their homework in on time. We had regular spelling tests, just to keep standards up to scratch, and we'd be expected to learn things by heart—it might be a Shakespearean sonnet or a piece of poetry. It all helped to develop your memory (a vital skill for passing exams), but it introduced us to the beauty of the written or spoken word and left many of us with a deep love of all things literary. 'Quinquereme of Ninevah, from distant Ophir' still sends shivers down my spine 50 years on. And I can still remember most of it.

But joy, for me at least, was brief. Every evening

there was homework to do after school, starting with a gentle hour in your first year of senior school and building up to a whopping three and a half hours per night for older pupils coming up to national exams, with extra projects that had to be completed during the school holidays and at weekends. The idea, so we were told, was to get us used to the idea of working under pressure and being self-reliant. Each term there would be an in-school exam, to accustom us to the formal examination room with its air of tension, and papers that had to be completed on time (no continuous assessment, course work or downloading essays from the Internet in those days). Then came mock O levels at 15 and the real thing at 16, followed by A levels for the most gifted pupils who were aiming to go to university. Only a small percentage of the brightest, most academic kids did in those days. Everyone else either went on to a technical college to learn a skill (art school and secretarial school were always particularly popular) or they became apprenticed to a tradesman to learn plumbing, carpentry or electrical work while earning their keep by doing the job hands on.

School plays were regular events. Infant and junior schools always put on a nativity play each Christmas. There'd be a lot of petty jealousies about who played the star roles of Joseph and Mary or one of the three wise men (second best), and who'd just be the back end of the donkey or the fifteenth shepherd in one of the crowd scenes. The real purpose was for as many kids as possible to play a part, so no one felt left out. As a last resort any small kids without 'proper' parts would be dressed up as sheep. By the time we reached secondary school, school plays became quite sophisticated, and we'd often tackle Shakespeare—abridged, of course.

Acting was ideal for those of us who liked to unleash our latent thespian talents; on stage it had adult approval instead of earning the usual 'now then, no showing off'. It was thanks to the art and drama teacher David Wildman that I first joined the Ilkley Players; I was given a part in *The Little Hut*, by André Roussin, which was considered a bit risqué. Mr Wildman took the precaution of sending a note home to my parents to see if they'd mind. The play was, he said, 'a little outspoken'. (I sneaked a look at the letter on the way home.) Anyway, my parents gave their blessing, and they needn't have worried. My part was the monkey who comes on at the very end, and I didn't even have a line of dialogue to speak, though I did get to throw some nuts at the principal characters. But that's the moment I dropped my dreams of becoming an engine driver and decided to be an actor instead. For a while . . .

Games and pastimes

Organized games were a big part of the school curriculum; they were thought to be character-forming and to help pupils develop leadership skills, besides getting us out in the fresh air to run around. Senior schools still had proper sports fields, of course—they hadn't yet been sold off for housing estates. Boys' schools played cricket in summer and football in winter (rugby if it was a posher school or a grammar school) while girls' schools played rounders in summer and hockey in winter, and you were jolly well expected to get out there and do your best, in all weathers. Swimming pools and tennis courts didn't exist at most 'normal' schools at the time. A few kids would have a knock-up with tennis rackets on the courts down by the river, which would be a brief craze every year just around Wimbledon fortnight, but it was mostly played—for want of a better word—against a 'net' drawn in chalk on the bus-garage wall at the end of our road. It was considered quite something for a school to have a gymnasium with a bit of basic kit like wall bars and a vaulting horse or a few ropes to climb. 'Gym' usually meant physical jerks, performed in a singlet and running shorts. But we also did a bit of cross-country running, out over the moors on silvery sandy tracks through the heather, which was wonderful. Like natural history on the hoof.

But that wasn't all the fresh air we got. Pupils had to get outside at break and again in the dinner hour. At senior school kids were expected to behave in a reasonably grown-up way so there wasn't too much larking about, but at primary school we took part in all sorts of unofficial playground games such as tag, conkers, jacks or marbles, and in the case of girls, skipping or hopscotch. You didn't play the same thing all year round; different games came and went in temporary crazes that swept the school, then you moved on to something else. Traditional playground games have vanished now that kids have mobile phones and hand-held computer-games consoles, and today's sophisticated schoolchildren would think them terribly uncool.

Conkers was one of my favourites and was, obviously, extremely seasonal. Small boys would keep a watchful eye on nearby horse chestnut trees

129

on their way home from school in the autumn term, so that as soon as the first fat, round, spiky green cases started to fall, we could help things along with a few well-aimed sticks or stones. Once on the ground any conker case that hadn't burst on impact would be opened by squashing it under your foot to extract the hard shiny spherical brown nut inside. The trick was to find a big beefy conker, then drill a hole through it and tie it to a string about a foot long. Boys would dry a likely-looking conker out in the oven or pickle it in vinegar to toughen it up. Then, dangling your carefully prepared specimen from the end of its string, you and your opponent took it in turns to clout the other one. The winning conker went on to play against others, notching up successes as it went. A 'sixer' was the survivor of six games, but if you beat another conker that was a 'niner' you would add that score to your own. I had a forty-sixer, a very venerable survivor that I'd treated to a dose of both oven and vinegar. I thought it was invincible, till I met up with a lad who secretly switched his conker for a steel nut on a string which shattered my hardened veteran at the very first swing.

Pea-shooters were another passing craze, and you made your own. Boys would use a penknife to cut dry stems of hogweed or, better still, Japanese knotweed from roadside verges on their way to or from school; if you caught them at just the right stage the pith inside had dried out leaving a rigid hollow tube, which formed a natural peashooter. You'd either 'borrow' a few dry peas from the pantry at home or buy a packet from a general store if you had lots of pocket money, and by loading a single pea into the tube and huffing violently you could score a direct hit on another boy's legs. As he'd have been wearing shorts, you could be sure it would sting. To be honest, pea-shooters didn't always go down terribly well in school playgrounds, and they'd often be confiscated by teachers—but since it only took seconds to make a new one, keen pea-shootists simply rearmed themselves on the way home. Once the hogweed stems became too dry and brittle, the pea-shooter season was over for another year. You could buy tin ones, but that was cheating . . .

Marbles or 'alleys' were played with in summer—rolling them across patches of the playground and claiming any others that you hit in the process. 'Holey' involved sending them into a hole scraped in the dried mud. Jacks were a summer sport, too—the little steel three-dimensional crosses that were flipped from the palm to the back of the hand while a small rubber ball was bounced on the ground in between picking them up. Cat's cradle was played at any time of year with a loop of string that could be turned into elaborate shapes between the hands of the dexterous.

Kick-can, though far too raucous for the school playground, was played at the bottom of the street, next to the bus garage wall. It was basically a game of hide-and-seek in which the hiders had to come out from their hiding places and kick an empty pea or bean can before the 'seeker' could do so first.

Hopscotch was for girls. You needed a stone, a piece of chalk and a clear area of playground. Someone (usually the biggest or bossiest girl) marked the distinctive shape on the playground with a piece of chalk and numbered the squares—1 to 12—then dropped a stone, usually

131

a flat piece of slate, on the first square. Then the player would hop from square to square, avoiding the square with the stone, but picking it up on her way back. Once she'd successfully negotiated the course to the end, the stone was moved up one place and the course was repeated, again missing out the square with the stone. So it went on till the stone reached square number 12 and the hopper hadn't missed her footing or fallen over. I never really saw the point in it myself, but then little girls and little boys never saw eye to eye on so many things.

Skipping was something else girls did. Some girls would skip on their own using a short skipping rope with wooden handles, but a lot of them also did it in a group using a long thin rope (which was often a bit of old washing line). Two jumps between turns of the rope would be 'normal' skipping, one jump between turns would be 'peppers' and two turns between each jump would be 'bumps'. The really athletic would go for 'double bumps'—three turns of the rope before landing. At this stage the lads became interested because failure could lead to spectacular falls and a glimpse of knickers.

With one girl at each end, turning vigorously with their arms rotating in large circles, the rope would be turned in a large arc and all the other girls would jump in, jump over the rope a few times and jump out, accompanied by various skipping rhymes, which us lads thought really rather silly. One I vaguely recall had a verse that went: 'Jelly on the plate, jelly on the plate, wibble wobble, wibble wobble, jelly on the plate.' High literature indeed.

CHAPTER 6

THE WAY WE WERE AT WORK

Long hours, short holidays and distinctly basic facilities were what people expected from their working life while I was growing up. It would be wrong to suggest that everybody enjoyed their job, and yet, in spite of the fact that many of them had little choice in the career they pursued, the vast majority did take pride in their work. The thing is that folk were rather better, in the main, at pacing themselves. With at least 50 years of manual labour ahead they worked steadily, rather than opting for city burn-out as is often the case today. Men stayed with the same firm for most of their working life, starting at the bottom and working their way to the top, or at least further up the ladder. There was loyalty on both sides and, with the benefit of hindsight, relative security, too.

Most of what we used to call ordinary working folk had jobs in shops, farms, mills and factories, and young lads were taken on as apprentices to learn trades like plumbing, joinery or engineering. It makes me smile when folk complain nowadays that they can't find a plumber, and that when they do the hourly rates are outrageously high. My dad was a plumber. He died in 1986 and had never taken home a three-figure sum in his weekly wage packet. Had he lived longer he might have benefited from the fact that when everybody goes to university the necessary craftsmen are thinner on the ground and perhaps more appreciated. So long as they don't ask too much for the job.

In most cases, only youngsters from educated middle-class backgrounds—in those days the elite—went to university. Oh, there had been cases of working-class men and women going to 'Oxbridge' way back in the twenties and thirties, and more frequently after the War, but it was very much the exception rather than the rule. The university educated were the ones who would be in line for the top jobs in the civil service and education, but commuting also allowed new opportunities in sales, advertising, publishing, TV and radio.

There wasn't the same emphasis on careers for girls. Sexist and non-PC though it may sound today, a lot of girls only expected to work till they got married and started a family. They planned on going back to work when their children were old enough to allow them more freedom during the day, which explains why they usually went in for jobs like teaching, office work, secretarial duties or hairdressing. These were occupations which could be taken up and put down according to family commitments, and if the husband had to move to a new location when he had a promotion, it was naturally assumed the wife would be only too happy to change jobs, keep domestic matters safely under control and generally play a supportive role behind the scenes, to further his career prospects.

Women did not have equal rights or anything of the sort; they were often paid only half as much as men—even when they were doing the same jobs—and they had very few managerial opportunities, largely because bosses assumed that they wouldn't stay long. In any case, men would never have taken

134

to being told what to do by a woman boss.

Pay day was Friday, and your wages—in notes and coins—were handed to you in a buff envelope four inches square with the amount visible in a window on the front and holes punched in the back so you could count the coins before opening. It was taken home by the man and, in our household at any rate, given to the wife who would hand back his 'pocket money' for the week. Dad never baulked at the prospect, bless him.

In those class-riddled days there was an enormous social gap between 'white-collar workers', with indoor jobs, and 'blue-collar workers' who worked with their hands. My family seemed to straddle both camps. My Uncle Jim, Dad's older brother, worked in a shoe shop; on my mother's side Uncle Herbert was a greengrocer over in Otley and Uncle Bert (the one with the Dormobile) was a grocer in Burley-in-Wharfedale. Being a plumber, my dad hoped that while not necessarily following directly in his footsteps I would at least become a joiner (I was good with my hands) and have 'a trade'. It was clear to my parents by the time I was 15 that an academic career was unlikely. I claim to have been a late developer; they would probably have explained that I 'just wasn't bright enough'. Either way, university was never an option, and with my scholastic career being less than spectacular, it was agreed that I could leave at 15, before sitting my GCEs (apart from art, which I passed a year early) and take up the offer of an apprenticeship in the local parks department nursery, gardening being my passion. Luckily the headmaster convinced my dad to let me give it a go, much against his better judgement. I muse, sometimes, on what would have happened if I'd stayed on. But not very often . . .

Manufacturing industries

When I was growing up, manufacturing was what Britain did best. Steel, shipbuilding, coal-mining, the potteries, paper and textile mills were all thriving, especially in the north. In the Midlands and 'down south' aircraft manufacturing and car factories were the up-and-coming industries, and all round the coast our ports and docks were booming. Factories were going flat out producing a wide range of consumer goods, which were in big demand after years of wartime shortages. A good many works were still owned by wealthy families who'd passed them down through generations from father to son, starting from Victorian times. They were usually known by the owner's name to which the words 'and sons' had been tacked on, long after the original founder's great-grandsons had inherited the factory. Tall chimney stacks were a familiar part of the skyline round industrial towns, since factories often had their own coal-burning power plant grafted on to one side. The smoke, stink and pollution were dreadful. Smog was a common feature of industrial towns and cities, compounded by coal-burning fires from all the rows of houses. London was the worst of the lot and pea-soupers through which it was difficult to breathe, let alone find your way home, were frequent.

Between them, the manufacturing industries employed a huge amount of people, and whole communities grew up round factories. Close to

Mills like this cotton factory in Lancashire thrived.

home we had the mill towns of Keighley, Silsden and Addingham, where Mum had once worked for Lister's. Like most mill-workers at the time she wore overalls and below them clogs, which protected your feet every bit as well as today's steel-toe-capped industrial boots, and they almost never wore out, thanks to the 'irons'—slender 'horseshoes' nailed to each sole and heel that were replaced at intervals.

Factories were everywhere; and the one good thing about working in them, as opposed to working at 'outdoor jobs' such as farming, was that the hours were usually quite regular. People would work from 8 till 5 or 9 till 5.30, and the factory hooter would signal the beginning and the end of the working day. Workers clocked on and off with a punch card, so the management could keep tabs on everyone's punctuality; if you turned up even ten minutes late, you'd have your pay docked by the appropriate amount. Many factories had their offices at one end of the building, partitioned off from the main factory area, but with no fancy facilities like carpets, blinds or insulation. Conditions were a bit primitive—hot in summer, cold in winter, and very noisy all the time. Workers would develop their own sign language to get over the din, and would mouth their words very clearly without making a sound. Les Dawson made a career out of imitating them!

Factories would often have their own team of travelling sales representatives out on the road selling their goods to other businesses, and at first they set out to visit their customers by bus or on bikes, though a company car soon became a regular perk of the job once fewer salesmen had to cover larger territories. But a smart appearance was always essential; for years you could recognize travelling salesmen or commercial travellers (as they were known) by their 'uniform' of suits, waistcoats, highly polished shoes and bowler hats, which many firms still insisted they wear long after most city commuters had given them up.

Work on the factory floor might have been a bit repetitive, but it was regular money and regular hours, and a bit of social life went with it. A lot of factories in the north closed down completely for a week or two each summer so that essential maintenance work could be done on the machinery, and everyone had to take their holiday at this time. These were known as wakes weeks, which usually

138

fell in the last week of July and the first week of August, and as a treat factories would often lay on charabanc outings for their workers to places like Blackpool. (This old tradition was the start of organized coach tours.) Factories had their own sports and social clubs, with cricket teams that played in the local leagues, or a work's brass band that performed at local events, and at Christmas there'd be children's parties to look forward to. They also had regular visits from mobile X-ray machines, screenings for TB, which was still rampant at the time, and blood donor units came round so that people could give blood in their lunch hours, but 'health and safety' as we know it today hardly existed. It makes you wonder how we survived.

Office work

Banks and insurance companies were huge employers, and jobs with them were highly sought after because, besides having more prestige and security (those were the days), they provided far more comfortable working conditions and better facilities than those in the offices at mills or factories. They'd often have their own canteen where the staff could take a civilized lunch break (a whole three-quarters of an hour!), instead of making do with a factory tea lady wheeling round a trolley of cheese sandwiches and an urn of stewed tea. And there would be a staffroom with lockers where the workers could keep their hats, coats and shopping bags. But standards were high. Female office staff were expected to look the part: skirt and blouse, twinset and pearls worn with court shoes—

trousers, even smart ones, were definitely out.

Offices were not particularly glamorous places; typists and clerks worked in one enormous barn-like room with wooden desks, all arranged in neat rows with just enough room to walk between them. Only managers had their own individual offices and even those were usually a row of small cramped 'cupboards' with doors opening off a central corridor. You had to be quite a senior manager in a big organization to get a large office with a swivel chair, a second window, a good view, or curtains instead of blinds—any trimmings of that sort instantly marked you out as one of the top bosses. The Civil Service had strict guidelines as to the entitlements of each layer of management—size of desk, number of filing cabinets, comfort of chair and whether or not a piece of carpet was allowed. Perhaps they still do.

Offices needed enormous numbers of staff because everything had to be done manually; it took perhaps 50 to 60 people to do the same amount of work that an IT-literate office worker does with a desktop computer and phone today. Each section (sales, accounts, general enquiries, orders, purchasing, etc) would have its own overall manager, and there would also be an office manager in charge of the clerical staff—normally an absolute tyrant, who didn't permit any slacking or taking time off for chit-chatting. Some clerks simply processed information, and there were filing clerks who kept copies of correspondence, forms, orders and invoices, and most importantly filed everything so it could be retrieved when needed. (The filing departments consisted of rows of metal filing cabinets stretching way into the distance.)

Accounts were written up by hand in enormous ledgers by accounts clerks, all very accurate but distinctly Dickensian—the books had to balance to the last penny, or else.

Apart from the very top bosses, no one had a phone on their desk. All incoming calls to the firm were answered by the in-house operator, so there was no worry about people wasting time making or receiving personal calls at work—it just couldn't happen. Even bosses had to have their calls put through via the operator; there simply wasn't the technology to dial direct to anywhere in the country. But it didn't matter because orders weren't placed over the phone; most sales were made in person with the firm's representatives, or by letter.

Not surprisingly, huge numbers of office staff were fully occupied dealing with correspondence of one sort or another. Each letter took a deal of time to write, and each department had a huge pool of typists. Bosses dictated letters to their own personal secretaries, who took them down word for word in faultless Pitman shorthand (which looked like rows of squiggles), then typed up the result. After doing a 'draft', so the boss could make any corrections and alterations, they'd type out a 'good' copy along with up to six carbon copies, to be filed for future reference. You couldn't just press a button; carbon copies were made by inserting sheets of blue carbon paper between sheets of copy paper into a manual sit-up-and-beg typewriter and bashing away hard enough for it to come through right to the bottom copy. The noise of clacking keys in a busy open-plan office was positively ear-splitting.

Other career opportunities

Big stores in large cities needed lots of assistants, and not surprisingly they had rather more sophisticated staff than the sort you found working behind the counters in village shops. Big department stores were still very *Are You Being Served?*, with a strict hierarchy of staff who could recognize 'the gentry' instantly and addressed account customers by name—and always very deferentially. Aside from showing due respect, it raised the tone of the whole establishment if other customers overheard a few 'your ladyships' and suchlike terms being sprinkled around. In the really 'posh' shops even the staff had to call each other Mr this or Miss that; Christian names were considered far too familiar, especially when customers were within earshot. Good grooming, superb manners and discreet service were essential qualifications. A few of the staff in 'gents' outfitting' might be decidedly fey—not the sort you'd want to be with in a cramped little cubicle measuring your inside leg—but no matter. Most of them knew to ask you to hold the intimate end of the tape measure.

Big stores would groom trainee managers, selected from large numbers of ambitious applicants, by moving them round each department in turn to give them a wide experience before they started to move up through the ranks. But shopwork was still shopwork, and even people who worked in the posh stores were expected to work Saturdays, though they often had a half day off for early closing during the week, usually on a Wednesday. Half day closing! Now there's a thing.

142

Most shopworkers are expected to be there for the start of the sales on Boxing Day nowadays. The prospect of losing half a day's trade midweek would make most shopkeepers go pale.

Nursing was a prestigious vocation and a great favourite for girls leaving school. A Nursing training gave a girl a good grounding for future life as a wife and mother, besides being the sort of job she could take up almost anywhere in the country. A lot of young trainee nurses secretly hoped that (rather like air hostesses) they might meet someone 'eligible' through their work— ideally a handsome doctor or a wealthy private patient with a none-too-serious ailment. Some no doubt did. Although girls needed a fair education and 'the right qualities' to be accepted, there were plenty of openings for nurses because in those days wards were heavily staffed with a mixture of student and qualified nurses of various grades, who all lived in the adjacent nurses' home. Overseeing them was a hierarchy of staff nurses and sisters all living in terror of a gimlet-eyed matron of the Hattie Jacques school who brooked no nonsense. Discipline was strict; wards were segregated into Men's or Women's—none of your modern mixed nonsense—and either medical, surgical or maternity depending on the nature of your particular affliction.

Every day the wards were thoroughly cleaned (carbolic was a byword), flowers arranged, lockers tidied and dusted, bed pans doled out, screens shifted and meals dispensed, all by the nurses in person, and doctors did their rounds regularly in white coats with stethoscopes round their necks. If you were a patient you'd be allowed no more than two visitors at a time, and then only during official visiting hours, which were short. When the bell rang for closing time visitors were ushered smartly out, then the wards were immediately cleaned to remove any traces of contamination brought in from 'outside'. Everything was spotless. You entered hospital to be cured of infections, not to pick them up.

Teaching was another favourite career, but you still needed a degree, and at the end of your university course you needed to spend an extra year learning how to teach a class of children as well. (That much holds good today.) There were plenty of jobs; the country needed a lot of teachers to cope with the post-war baby boom. Every village had its own primary school, and every town had its own grammar and secondary schools. Classes could sometimes be quite large. A teacher would be expected to cope with maybe 35 to 50 children without any extra help, but it wasn't as bad as it sounds because a lot of learning was done by rote (the times tables, for instance), and in the 1950s children were brought up to have good manners and respect their elders, so there were fewer troublemakers. In any case, the cane, the ruler or the strap were all still used to mete out instant on-the-spot justice, so kids learned it was generally wiser to toe the party line and behave in class, even if they did lark about a bit on the way to and from school. For most of them a clout from the teacher would mean another clout at home, not the initiation of an internal inquiry with the board of governors.

The telephone exchange was another big employer; every big town had one. There was no trunk dialling at first—phones didn't have a dial, you lifted the receiver and rattled it up and down to call the operator (invariably a girl), and then asked her to connect you to the exchange and number you wanted. She'd be sitting with a headset on, in front of a massive bank of terminals into which she'd plug a cable to connect each call. Direct dialling (STD) didn't come in until 1958 and was not completed countrywide until 1979. It made all the difference to callers in a hurry because you could connect straight through to anywhere in the country, but it caused the closure of a lot of telephone exchanges. It's an odd thing, though; as communications became faster and easier, we all found a lot more to talk about so we all spent far longer on the phone. It took over from the village pump or post office as the purveyor of general gossip.

But by the time I'd left home and moved to London to take up my place as a student at Kew, the swinging sixties were upon us and all sorts of glamorous new jobs were opening up for girls. Tall, leggy, good-lookers were heading for careers such as modelling, and at modelling schools they'd be taught charm and deportment, and how to get in and out of a sports car elegantly while wearing a miniskirt without showing too much leg. (The secret, evidently, was to sit and swivel with your knees firmly clamped together.) Daughters of wealthy society parents—the sort who might once upon a time have come out as 'debs'—would be sent off to finishing school. It was rather smart; they'd learn essential life skills, such as etiquette, cookery and flower arranging, for making and maintaining a good marriage—which was for life, unlike a career which was probably only going to be for a few years. Funny how the two became interchangeable in time frame. But a modelling course in swinging London was a good 'extra' while they waited for Mr Right, and great fun you can bet, even if they never became the next Twiggy or Jean Shrimpton.

Learning on the job

After formal schooling came to an end, there was no time or money to waste on gap years, travel or 'finding yourself'. School-leavers from working-class backgrounds needed to get a job straight away since their parents couldn't afford to keep them any longer. But there were ways of earning a living at the same time as learning a trade.

Lads would apply for apprenticeships with established companies from local plumbing or joinery firms to large engineering concerns such as Rolls-Royce. The idea was that in return for a thorough on-the-job training, you'd accept a low wage and spend your spare time studying for exams.

Apprenticeships offered a way in to trade for young men. Army apprenticeships provided another route.

With my parents in Ilkley.

The whole family on the day of
my christening in 1949.

Everyone made their meals from scratch so the pantry was always well stocked.

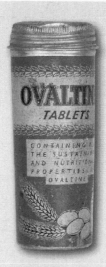

Margarine was a cheap alternative to butter.

We didn't
need much
to keep busy
for a day on
the beach.

All the grandmas loved the bingo.

B	I	N	G	O
11	22	45	54	61
1	26	44	46	67
3	18	FREE SPACE	51	62
14	20	37	50	71
7	23	41	53	72

The old
Routemaster buses
on Oxford Street.

On the new diesel
trains passengers
passed the time in a
most civilized manner.

Car-themed
cigarette cards.

One of the
glamorous
air hostesses
employed
to take your
mind off
the fear
of flying.

All over the world B.O.A.C. takes good care of you

BRITISH OVERSEAS AIRWAYS CORPORATION

The Boeing 707—the first of the big jet airliners.

No farmyard was complete without a few hens scratching about.

Horses were the powerhouses of many farms.

Me (standing third from the left at the front) at nursery school—three afternoons a week before starting 'proper' school aged five.

The chemistry lesson—a source of excitement at senior school.

Skipping was something girls did while chanting
rhymes, which us lads thought was rather silly.

Young apprentices
learned the ropes from
older, experienced
tradesmen.

Society girls were often sent off to finishing school to complete their education. They'd learn essential life skills, such as cookery, flower arranging and deportment.

Factory workers clocked on at the start and finish of their shifts.

Every high street had a butcher's shop.

Matchbooks carried advertising for local businesses and national brandnames like Lyons.

Me with Grandma Titch in one of her floral day dresses, and my sister, Kath.

Me in cowboy mode in the back garden.

Comics like *Hotspur* would keep us kids happy for hours.

It was perfectly safe mucking about in the streets. We would make a game out of whatever we could fin lying around.

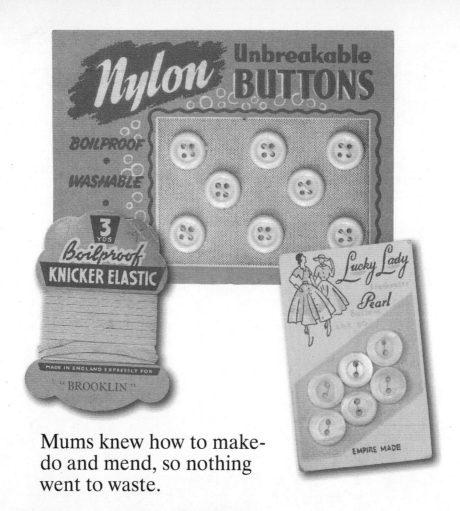

Mums knew how to make-do and mend, so nothing went to waste.

There were all sorts of contraptions to help mums in the kitchen.

Agatha
Christie's
*The
Mousetrap.*

Pasta
was an
exciting
new type
of food
people
were
beginning
to
discover
on their
foreign
holidays.

The Coronation
procession
travelled
through the
streets of
London which
were lined with
well-wishers.

A Coronation issue ladies' compact.

The whole country celebrated the Coronation with street parties and rallies.

The Queen with Oba Adele at Yaba, Nigeria in 1956.

The Queen opens Parliament in 1958.

You'd sign up for five years and be moved round every department learning all the various skills in each under the watchful eye of an experienced senior worker or departmental manager. He'd report back on your progress, then after you'd passed your exams, and if they thought you were good enough, the firm would offer you a permanent job. Not surprisingly, by the time a young chap had been through all that to learn his chosen trade, he tended to stick with it for life. Otherwise it meant moving back to the bottom of the ladder just when he'd started 'to get somewhere' and earn decent money—and since by then he'd be married with a family on the way, a fresh start was out of the question as he'd need all his new-found income to meet rapidly rising expenditure. The little woman would have made quite sure of it.

The armed services were still huge employers at the time; even though the War had ended, the Cold War was in full swing. For lads leaving school the services were the best way to see the world, have some adventures and learn a useful skill they could use back in Civvy Street afterwards. A lot of airline pilots, cooks, policemen, transport engineers and depot managers came from armed services backgrounds. Lads might go straight from school to a recruiting office to join up, or end up there after making a false start at another career. Potential officers, who were often people from long-standing military families following in father's footsteps, went to the big military training schools of Dartmouth (for the navy), Sandhurst (for the army) or Cranwell (for the RAF). Successful career officers could stay in the service till retirement age at 55—early by other employment standards.

TIME OFF

A lot of people were expected to work not just Monday to Friday but all day or half a day on Saturday as well, so Sunday was their only regular day off, and any extra days were very welcome.

Apart from your summer holiday (which was only one week, never two for the working classes, and usually had to be taken at the time of your employer's choosing), the only other time off people had were official bank holidays such as Whitsun (replaced since 1967 with the Late Spring Bank Holiday), Good Friday, Easter Monday, and August Bank Holiday. At Christmas everyone worked till the close of business on Christmas Eve (I can remember Dad coming home looking distinctly squiffy after a 'quick drink to celebrate' after they'd finished the last customer late one Christmas Eve—Mum was not amused). Everyone had Christmas and Boxing Days off, but then they were back at work as usual the day after—none of this stretching Christmas out over two weeks. There was a New Year's Eve party to look forward to when I was a nipper since Yorkshire is fairly close to Scotland. But down south even that was quite low key, and in England New Year's Day wasn't a public holiday at the time.

But for a secondary-school student with one O level in art, green fingers and a fondness for 'showing off' on stage, gardening was the only serious choice—especially given his secret ambition to be like his big horticultural hero, Percy Thrower. Though I didn't know it at the time, a series of lucky coincidences meant I was about to embark on a long unofficial apprenticeship for a gardening media career that I couldn't have planned if I'd tried.

The education of a gardener

When I left school I went straight into a job as an apprentice gardener at Little Lane Nursery, where the Ilkley Parks Department had its greenhouses. It was in the first week of August 1964 and just a ten-minute bike ride from home. I was put in the care of the parks foreman, Ken Wilson, given three antique Victorian greenhouses to look after, and paid three pounds eight shillings and sixpence per week, most of which I gave to Mum for my keep. It's what was expected of anyone earning a wage who still lived at home—well, you couldn't expect to keep living there for free.

It was heaven. After all those mind-numbing hours sitting at a school desk, I can't tell you how liberating it felt to have all day to tend the potted geraniums and celosias, and the plants for the council's bedding schemes. I stayed for four years, learning my way round all the routine jobs: sowing seeds, taking cuttings, potting plants, digging, mixing and sterilizing John Innes composts and stoking the boiler that heated the hot-water pipes that kept the greenhouses warm in winter. I was eventually trusted to take charge of the showy pot plants used for displays in the public library and the town hall. I even helped with the floral decorations for the highlight of Ilkley's social life, the Civic Ball. I went off with a huge vanload of chrysanths, ferns and hydrangeas, and banked them up round the stage, balcony and boxes. The effect was like a fairyland.

But being an apprentice I wasn't allowed to escape further education altogether. I was sent off to study horticulture at day-release classes in nearby Shipley, and most of my evenings were spent at home studying for my City and Guilds exams. To my amazement I discovered I didn't mind a bit of 'book-learning' when it meant studying something I was interested in. I even coped quite well with the Latin plant names, which I fixed in my head by writing them out time after time—like lines—and then, when I was desperate, setting them to music and singing them. Usually to 'La donna è mobilé'. Well, it seemed to work.

After four years of sheer horticultural bliss, 'ambition' put an end to Little Lane Nursery. There were regrets, but I felt it was time to spread my wings. I applied to go to college, but since the local one—Askham Bryan near York—didn't have a place for me that year, I moved south to Oaklands near St Albans in Hertfordshire. This time I was studying commercial horticulture (which covers market gardens, greenhouse crops and wholesale plant production) as opposed to the amenity sort (decorative bedding plants and floral displays) that I'd done so far. At Oaklands we learnt all about budding, grafting and pests, and we had weekly plant-identification tests. We were also taught how to use a library properly to undertake serious research on any horticultural topic—just how big a godsend that was to be in later life as a gardening journalist I had no idea at the time.

At the end of the nine-month course, armed with my National Certificate in Horticulture, I applied for a place on the three-year diploma course at the Royal Botanic Gardens, Kew. Each year, out of hundreds of would-be students, they accepted just 20. And they took me. I was thrilled. It wasn't just that Kew was a brilliant place to be—they had (and still have) probably the best living plant collection in this country, if not the world—I felt enormously lucky.

Being a student at Kew was not like doing a conventional college course, with three terms each year divided by holidays. No, each year was made up of three months of lectures followed by nine months' work in the gardens. We still had weekly plant-identification tests, but these were decidedly challenging since the plants put out for us to name could be taken from anywhere within Kew's vast collections of rarities. Over the three years, students were moved round all the different departments at Kew, gaining experience in each, under the guidance of the assistant curators. Besides practical gardening tasks we learned landscape construction and design, botany (plant anatomy, physiology, genetics and the science of naming), mycology (fungi, particularly the sort that cause plant disease) and entomology (bugs). We even studied subjects as far-flung as meteorology. Well, weather has a big bearing on gardening, not least when you want to know whether or not to wear your mac to work. And when all else fails,

151

every good gardener knows they can always blame the weather, so a fair understanding of it always pays off.

Kew made an enormous impression on me. It was while learning to grow orchids in the tropical houses that I developed a deep and abiding loathing for cockroaches. Hordes of these enormous black brutes lived under the stones outlining the paths, and they were always getting underfoot first thing in the morning, before visitors arrived, when we went in to water the plants. Oh, I knew it was irrational; they weren't going to hurt me. But there's something singularly loathsome about the brisk 'crunch' when you step on one, and the squish of horrible creamy goo squirting out of the flattened body while the antennae continue waving. I've gone out of my way to avoid them ever since. I also had the rather dubious pleasure of looking after the oldest pot plant in the world, the cycad originally collected by Francis Masson (one of Kew's most famous and successful plant-hunters) in 1775. I was terrified it might choose to pop its clogs during my watch, and I'd get the blame, so I was relieved to move on to new duties.

It was at Kew that I first fell in love with alpines. In my final year I was able to spend a three-week working 'exchange visit' abroad at the Munich Botanic Garden's alpine garden high up in the Bavarian Alps. Although it was early summer, it was freezing cold at night and rained as regular as clockwork every afternoon, yet the high peaks all around us were covered in snow. Most of the work consisted of weeding beds of tiny treasures and top-dressing between them with grit, even in downpours. Luckily, the alpine meadows and the

152

plants in the landscaped collection were at their peak, which was a breathtaking sight.

My three years at Kew were brilliant for notching up concentrated plant knowledge and wide-ranging practical experience, but at last I was ready for my first proper job. As luck would have it, Kew needed someone to take over as supervisor of the Queen's Garden (the seventeenth-century bit tucked away behind Kew Palace). I applied and got the job. I reckoned it would allow me to learn more about Kew's fabulous plants while earning some money. But fate took a hand, and, at the last minute, Kew's new curator, John Simmons, offered me the opportunity to carve out an entirely new job, setting up staff training courses from scratch, which would mean doing a lot of the teaching and practical demonstrations myself. After years of acting and singing in various operatic and theatrical groups—including one I'd joined while I was at Kew—I quite fancied the idea of being 'on stage' in front of an audience of students. I said yes.

Moving into the media

That was great for a couple of years, but I found I wasn't looking forward to the idea of repeating the same set of talks and demonstrations all over again to an audience who were not always keen to learn. By a stroke of luck an interesting-sounding advert turned up in the job pages of a horticultural journal—the Hamlyn Publishing Group needed an assistant editor to work on their gardening books. I applied, and was taken on. And who should be one of their star authors but my idol, Percy Thrower.

The editorial staff in the gardening section

taught me all the finer points of editing copy, proofreading and commissioning photographs. They hammered home the importance of good grammar and accurate spelling and punctuation. I set to. Through the job I met many gardening greats of the time. I first worked with Percy Thrower when his classic Encyclopaedia of Gardening needed revising. I'd had a copy for years; it was my first real gardening book, bought for me as a Christmas present by my mother when I was knee-high. I worked with Percy again on his great fruit and veg bible, which meant making occasional trips up to his home, The Magnolias, just outside Shrewsbury. His gardening programmes were filmed from there, and in front of the cameras, he had the uncanny ability to say precisely what was needed, engagingly, with no waffle, and fit it exactly into the right length of time. He made it look so easy. It's not. At least to start with. I studied Percy's technique carefully and tried to develop one of my own. Well, as I knew from Kew it paid to learn what you could where you could, in case it came in useful one day.

Meanwhile, I'd started doing a little writing of my own. It all began when an author failed to deliver his manuscript for a book on house plants, so I stepped into the breach. By writing virtually all night, every night, I just finished by the allotted deadline. It was accepted, and shortly after I was asked to write another book on gardening under cover. I started doing a bit of writing for *Amateur Gardening* magazine, since my boss at Hamlyn had close connections with them.

After a couple of years of book-editing, that same boss suggested I might think about moving into magazines. He'd spotted I was growing restless and felt I was ready for the next new challenge. I joined *Amateur Gardening*, based in London, as assistant editor, and later became the magazine's deputy editor. It seemed like fate. By then I was newly married and was busy setting up home, so a move was the last thing I needed, with so much other expense. Meanwhile Percy Thrower retired, or as one of the newspapers put it was 'given the order of the welly boot', since he had started appearing in TV advertisements in contravention of the BBC's unwritten rules.

I'd often wondered how you went about getting into TV. In the *Amateur Gardening* office one day the sub-editor, Graham Clarke, said he'd received a letter a while previously from Radio 4's lunchtime consumer programme *You and Yours* asking if the magazine could recommend someone to do an occasional gardening item for them. He rummaged in his desk drawer and handed it over. I replied, and was telephoned a few weeks later and asked to record a short piece for the programme on turfing. Could this be my big break, I wondered? Well, not exactly, but it was a start.

The turning point in my career was the Great Greenfly Invasion of summer 1979. Aphids swarmed across the channel, smothering everything in their wake. The *Today* programme rang from Radio 4 and asked me to do a short piece advising on the best way to combat the marauding aphids. Later the same day *Nationwide* rang, wanting me to cover the same story again for them on TV in the evening. It seemed to go well and 'live' TV was hugely exciting. I came home full of excitement and gave the wife a blow-by-blow account.

I didn't hear from them again until a year later

when someone's roof garden crashed down through the ceiling into the flat below and they wanted me to chat about the right way to go about roof gardening. I was invited back to do a weekly spot for them. I was still appearing on Radio 4 every week—albeit for a total of four minutes—and was now doing a fair bit of writing at home which took up most of my evenings, all on top of the day job for Amateur Gardening. Something had to give.

Fate stepped in again. *Amateur Gardening* decided to move away from London to new offices in Poole, Dorset, and I felt—after all the work I'd done on the new house, and with our first baby on the way—I just couldn't face the upheaval of the move. I stayed put, gave up the regular paying job and turned freelance. *AG* were very good about it and gave me some feature writing to do for them, but I was on my own from then on. A big risk? Certainly. In those days people—especially men, who were still expected to be the breadwinners—trod carefully where careers were concerned and, if possible, joined a blue-chip firm, then spent years working their way up through the ranks. Anyone who chose to strike out on their own with no safety net could only expect what they got if it all went pear-shaped. But whatever life had in store for me I could at least look forward to spending more time with my wife and family.

CHAPTER 7

THE WAY WE WERE ON THE HIGH STREET

Funny how today you can survive without ever leaving the house—even when it comes to shopping. You can order, and a van will bring your goods. Short of saying a brief 'hello' to the driver you don't have to make contact with anyone. Not that it will do much for your social skills. But a trip to the shops was part of the daily routine for most 1950s housewives. With few fridges and no freezers people had to go out to buy fresh bread, meat and veg almost every day—usually on foot or by bus. Progress was slow for mothers with a small child on 'reins' and a baby in a pram; a bit of shopping could take all morning. No one shopped for fun— shopaholics didn't exist—money was tight, and in any case there weren't all that many consumer goods to buy. It was mostly bare essentials. If you wanted a new dress you went to the 'remnant shop' and bought the fabric, the cotton and the paper pattern. At least, that's what happened in our house, and Mum would spend her evenings cutting out the strange shapes on the rug in front of the fire, and then stitching them all together on the treadle-operated Singer sewing machine.

Tinned food counted as a luxury that was hoarded for emergencies. If you had visitors you'd open a tin of red salmon to make sandwiches, to show you could afford it, and the wartime standby, Spam, was still to be found in every kitchen cupboard along with corned beef, pilchards and

157

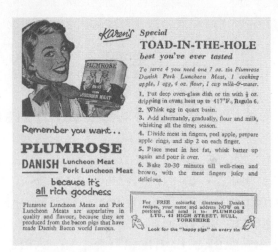

*Tinned luncheon meat—a luxury that
would be saved for emergencies.*

sardines—good emergency options. As for clothes, most people generally had three of everything (one on, one off and one in the wash), which we wore till they wore out and couldn't be mended any more. We'd go for an occasional shopping trip by train to Leeds, which was our nearest big town, but it was usually to buy 'serious stuff' such as a winter coat. Even our school uniforms came from the drapery department of the local Co-op.

The closest most fifties families came to a recreational shopping expedition was, that rarest of treats, a day's sightseeing to London. If you went, it was essential to bring home a few souvenirs. Few visitors to London could resist the inevitable fist-sized glass dome containing a model of the Houses of Parliament that whirled up a snowstorm when you shook it. Kept on show on the mantelpiece, it was a bit like having those luggage stickers that people became so fond of in the 1960s saying 'Cannes, Rimini and Nice'. It was nice to show you'd been.

High street shops

If you look at old black and white photos of high streets of 1950s towns, what strikes you straight away—apart from the distinct lack of cars—is how small, dark and dingy the shops are. You have to look hard to see what they sold, since they didn't have huge signs outside and their windows were small with no lights and just a few goods arranged very unimaginatively on the windowsill inside. There was nothing fancy; a ladies'-clothes-shop window would perhaps have a single frock on a headless mannequin, while a gent's outfitters might have a few sensible socks pulled onto plastic feet. Things weren't much better inside: there were no tasteful displays enticing you to buy; most of the stock was held in boxes stacked against the back wall or carefully folded and stowed under glass counters or in glass-fronted boxes that scaled the back wall of the shop. Half the time the assistant had to go to the stockroom out the back to find your size.

Some shops were household names that you'd know today. We had Boots the Chemist, Freeman, Hardy and Willis, the Army and Navy Stores, Dorothy Perkins and Woolworths, known as a 'variety store' since it sold so many different things under one roof. It was also known for offering good value. When I was a boy it had a series of counters—manned by assistants—each specializing in particular types of goods. Before the firm went to the wall it had become supermarket-like with checkouts at the exits. Back in the fifties the glamorous-looking counters—all chrome and glass—had folk serving behind them. There was one for sweets, another for cosmetics, and there were counters for lampshades, general hardware and sewing stuff, but the one I was most interested in was the gardening counter which had all sorts of useful sundries. Most of my pocket money went on seeds—Cuthberts and Bees were the F. W. Woolworth brands—and I was always intrigued by their rose bushes—the three or four foot-long stems tied together so they would fit into a narrow polythene sleeve, and the bare roots coiled around into a smaller bag of their own. 'Helen Traubel' and 'Piccadilly', 'Rose Gaujard' and 'Peace' were all bought for the front garden. And what's more, they lived and thrived! Every visit to Woolies brought new treasures to discover, and I'd hand over my coppers to the smiling sales assistant. It was just the same everywhere you went—personal service.

But most of the big high street names of the time have long since vanished. Lyon's Corner Houses could once be found in most big towns, dispensing tea and coffee, and cakes, snacks or light meals—Welsh rarebit and beans on toast—at affordable prices. Their waitresses wore severe uniforms and thick, pancake make-up which looked as if it would crack and fall off if they smiled. Cafés like these were the fast-food outlets of their day, except that a visit was more of an occasion and you ate in, at a table, properly laid with a cruet, knives and forks, and serviettes—there was no taking-away. In any case it would never have been 'done' to be seen eating in the street.

In Ilkley we had one smart café, up at the posh end of town on The Grove. The art-deco-inspired Bluebird café was where Grandma Titch worked as a 'nippy'—the name for waitresses at the more upmarket cafés who were famed for the speed at which they nipped about between tables and kitchens. In those days it was quite a skilled job since it involved 'silver service'. Instead of customers helping themselves from a side dish of veg put down on their table, the food was dispensed onto plates by a properly trained waitress using a spoon and fork in one hand and the dish in the other—a tricky manoeuvre that took a deal of learning. Get it wrong and you'd flick dollops of mash all over the tablecloth or lob a sausage into the customer's lap. Nippies also had to be able to deliver six plates of food at once, all balanced carefully along one arm. It took some doing. But Grandma Titch must have been pretty nifty at it, since she was still balancing plates and dispensing veg from paired spoons at the age of 76, when Dad suggested it might be time to think about taking life a bit easier. She reduced the plates to five.

The mainstay of any town high street was its vast range of small independent shops, which often arranged their wares in huge stacks outside on the pavement to increase their sales area and to act as advertising, even though each evening the whole lot had to be picked up and put back inside just before the shop closed. Greengrocers made a platform of old orange boxes topped with bright green papery grass that they unrolled over the top, like turf, on which they piled precarious pyramids of oranges, carrots, apples, onions and cabbages, each with prices—in old pence—on bits of paper impaled on wire prongs. Markets still do this today, of course, but pre-supermarkets it was the way all green comestibles were displayed for sale. Ironmongers (or hardware shops, as we'd call them today) were the spitting image of Ronnie Barker's shop in *Open All Hours*, with a glorious jumble of tin bathtubs, washboards, gardening tools, pudding basins, rolls of wire netting and cake tins arranged on the pavement outside.

Inside they'd have great big crates or buckets for loose nails, tin-tacks, washers, bolts and cup-hooks, which you bought in quantities ranging from a pound to a handful or just a few, which were wrapped up in a thick paper parcel or dropped into a brown paper bag to take home. There were none of today's prefilled, sealed and shrink-wrapped plastic bags that take hours to open and force you to buy 50 tin-tacks or half-inch screws when you only wanted two. They also sold loose seeds, weighed out from wooden cabinets in the back of the shop and decanted into thick brown paper bags with a little scoop. It was a very economical way to buy peas and beans, provided they were fresh.

Every high street also had a baker, who got up in the middle of the night so that by the time the first housewives ventured out he'd have warm crusty bread on the counter and rolls and buns on the shelves. He didn't need a large sign over his shop; the mouth-watering smell of new bread wafting down the high street was all the advertising he needed. Then there were butchers, whose window display would often feature something grisly like a whole pig's head, while the shop interior had trays of chops and mince alongside a giant wooden chopping block on which the butcher (kitted out afresh each morning in a crisp white apron which was soon splattered with blood) chopped your required cut of meat with a hatchet or a machete-sized knife from half a sheep or a hind-quarter of beef that he'd lift down from a hook. It was an impressive performance, especially seen against a background of strings of home-made sausages on hooks and whole freshly-plucked chickens hanging by their necks with the heads and feet still intact. Despite the gory displays that left no doubt in your mind that meat came from animals and not from plastic bags, vegetarians were virtually unheard of. Pork butchers were northern specialists who went in for fresh home-made pies, faggots, black puddings and similar delicacies, all made with the offcuts (for want of a better word) of the pig.

Another high-street essential was the haberdasher's, a sort of general store for sewing, knitting and dressmaking. They'd sell anything from a reel of cotton to zips, buttons, bodkins, ribbon, knicker-elastic, the special curved knitting needles for making socks or wooden darning mushrooms (which were pushed inside a sock while you mended a hole by weaving wool over the missing part). In those days housewives always mended holes and tears instead of buying new clothes, and went in for a good deal of knitting, sewing, crocheting and dressmaking, especially for baby clothes and girls' dresses, and they still embroidered their own tablecloths.

Banks were to be found on every high street, but in much smaller and plainer incarnations than those of today. Names like Martin's, National Provincial and the Yorkshire Penny Bank have long since been swallowed up by larger firms. Even small local branches had their own resident manager, who knew all his customers personally, by name. If you wanted to borrow money you went in to see him

TELEPHONES

Hardly anyone had their own phone at home when I was small, but you'd find telephone boxes in towns, strategically situated outside the main post office, in the square and on major corners. They were the proper red sort, which are mostly collectors' pieces now, used as garden gazebos. Goodness knows who people phoned, except for shops and businesses. But if you needed a plumber you could at least ring to book your burst pipes in for treatment, which is why ours was one of the first houses in our street to have a phone —Dad needed it for work. Ilkley 107 was the number, sadly just a digit off James Bond, but then Dad only had a licence to plumb.

At least by the time we got our phone, in the early 1960s, you could direct dial. People who had a phone at home in the 1950s often had the old upright 'candlestick' phones with handles which you banged up and down to summon the operator. When she replied, you'd dictate the exchange and number you wanted (Whitehall 1212, for instance, was Scotland Yard), and she'd then connect you. A phone was a great luxury to be used very sparingly—children and teenagers never used it without permission—and everyone kept calls short and to the point, with no idle chit-chat. A lot of people put on a special 'telephone voice' for answering the phone to impress whoever was at the other end with their refined tones.

STD (Subscriber Trunk Dialling) didn't

come in until 1958, and then only gradually, but it was seen as a huge advance since you dialled the number of the telephone switchboard followed by the number of the subscriber you wanted to speak to, and the call went straight through automatically. As the demand for household phones grew, 'party lines', where one line was shared between two houses, were introduced as a way of stretching limited resources round all the people who wanted to be connected. People would never know whether their neighbours were on the phone until they picked it up and heard a conversation already taking place. Good manners demanded that you put the phone down straight away, without listening in, and try again later, but there was no such thing as privacy. And how on Earth the telephone company worked out the bills I'll never know.

to ask for a loan—and then it would only be for something as sensible as a mortgage for a house, car or home improvements. There was no such thing as a credit card. He'd gravely enquire as to your earnings, outgoings and personal circumstances before deciding whether to advance you any money or not, and his word was law—there was no going into the red without permission. The first slight transgression would result in a sharp letter from the bank, straight away, and a bounced cheque was the height of embarrassment. You could always read stories about terrible rogues in the newspapers. (Well, there wasn't a lot of real crime to make the headlines, and papers rarely printed celebrity gossip—except the odd piece about Elizabeth Taylor, Diana Dors or Jayne Mansfield—society scandals or stories that showed politicians in a bad light. It wasn't done. All that came later in the 1960s.) Most people saw their bank manager as a respected family friend, even if it was the sort that always had a touch of headmasterly bossiness about him. You probably stayed with the same bank for most of your life. It was just the same with your family doctor and solicitor—they all knew you personally.

Small independent grocers' shops were widespread; when you went in, a bell on the door jangled so the assistants were on their toes ready for customers. Again it was all personal service; if the shop was full of other customers you'd queue until it was your turn to be served and then you'd ask for each item in turn from the shopping list you'd drawn up before leaving home. (This was considered essential to stop you from going home without something vital, but also to keep you from the perils of impulse buying, which would just have been a waste of money—and people didn't have it to spare.)

The assistant would lift tins or packets down from the packed shelves round the walls of the shop interior, climbing up a little ladder if need be. Bacon would be sliced to order using a fiendish machine with a gigantic rotating blade and a sliding rack on which half a side of bacon was impaled on a row of little spikes; when the handle was turned, the machine spat out perfect slices of bacon into a pile at one side which was carefully wrapped up in special greaseproof paper by hand. Coffee would be roasted and ground from real beans by a machine in the shop, and the haunting aroma would be piped outside through an extractor fan to draw customers in. And if you found it too inconvenient to go into town to visit the shop, the owner would visit once a week to take your order, writing everything down in his notebook. It was delivered—neatly packed in a cardboard box, with the washing powder wrapped separately in newspaper to prevent it from contaminating the food—the next day.

A 1950s town had a slow pace of life and a relaxed atmosphere. With so few cars, there was no call for car parks, traffic wardens or double yellow lines; the few people who came by car just left their vehicles along the kerb at the side of the road or parked nose-end-in at the main square in the centre of town. And all along the pavements would be benches where people could sit and have a rest, read the newspaper or just watch the world go by. There weren't many litter bins, but then people didn't eat in the street and they would never have dreamt of dropping litter—if they had any, they took it home with them.

Market towns

Market towns were a few sizes larger than usual, and there were two sorts. Livestock markets were still being held in many larger market towns right up to the late 1960s. The one in the Hampshire town where I now live managed to last until the early 1980s, but it was a rarity. A particular area just off the town centre would be filled with permanent pens made from heavy-duty steel bars, and on market day local farmers would bring their calves, cows, store cattle, sheep and pigs to sell once or twice a week. There would be a lot of other stalls as well, selling bits and bobs of agricultural gear. They were fascinating places for kids to explore, even if you risked a clip round the ear when you got in the way of stockmen and dealers. After closing time all the straw would be swept up and the area disinfected, so it was left clean till the next market day.

There would also be a huge street market, held near the centre of town, on a street which either didn't get too much traffic or could easily be closed off for the day. Smaller towns might have a weekly one too. Street markets aren't all that different today—a colourful shanty town of stalls selling greengrocery, clothing and all sorts of goods at rather less-than-shop prices. The big difference was that in the 1950s street traders still sold bananas by the pound, and they'd attempt to draw customers to their stand by yelling out their wares at the tops of their voices. Some traders, it has to be said, weren't entirely honest or totally sober, especially after lunch, since the pubs tended to stay open longer on market days, but it all added to local colour.

A vital ingredient of any street market was stalls selling hot food and drinks, and very welcome they were on cold winter days. Market regulars knew that the best way to keep your hands warm was by wrapping them round a mug of hot tea. Stalls also did good business selling bacon sandwiches and other delicacies such as saveloys, faggots and mushy peas—which were what passed for 'fast food', eaten sitting down at little tables and chairs set up all round the stall. A traditional market town still had a horse trough, a substantial affair made of sandstone, granite or even marble and parked in the centre of town where demand from thirsty animals would be greatest. By the late 1950s and early 1960s they'd lost most of their original function, so most of them had been filled with earth and planted with geraniums. But they were still there.

Nurseries

Garden centres were non-existent in the 1950s, but each town had one or two small family nurseries that grew their own plants and sold them direct to the public, and they were where most gardeners bought their plants. Ilkley had two, which I used regularly. Close to the centre of town was Mr Robertson's, a cluster of long, low, white-painted greenhouses nestling behind the police station, and further away, on the banks of the River Wharfe, was my favourite—the Old Bridge Nurseries. They were both what you'd call 'quaint' today. Like all small nurseries at the time they only stocked the most popular stuff that they could be sure to shift. Bedding plants were sold in wooden 'flats', something like today's plastic seed trays but made from thin strips of wood nailed together. (Today, old wooden seed trays are gardening antiques, found at fancy prices in bijou little shops and largely used for decorating posh outbuildings.)

Small plants such as alpines were sold in whatever was cheapest, perhaps thin white plastic vending cups, and if shrubs were sold in containers at all (which was still a great novelty at the time) they'd be set out for sale in rusty old tin cans— larger shrubs were put in empty jam or tomato catering tins that came from factory canteens. After a time, when container plants caught on more, shrubs were sold growing in thin black plastic bags. But while I was growing up most serious garden enthusiasts ordered all their trees, shrubs and roses from nurseries who grew them in rows in fields and dug them up during the winter. People would either go and visit the nursery fields in summer to choose which plants they liked, or they'd order by post from the sort of catalogue that consisted of lists of names without any pictures. It wasn't till the late 1960s that the idea of garden centres started to blossom: small family nurseries on the edges of towns started to buy in other people's plants, build a smart little shop and stock a few garden products.

The peak times for the nursery trade would be in that dormant season between November and March, when trees and shrubs were dug up from nursery rows and despatched for planting; in September when the wallflowers, polyanthus, sweet Williams and other spring bedding plants were sold; and the summer bedding season in late May—never beforehand, since any nurseryman worth his salt would not let you take home plants that would be at risk of being killed by frost. He valued your custom. He wanted you to return. And he wouldn't have a checkout—just a wooden box or an old biscuit tin.

'Old money' and decimalization

When I was at primary school, along with basic numeracy one of the many things that a small child had to learn about was money. It took some doing. In those days the currency had a lot of character; the notes were bigger, and the coins were thicker and heavier so they felt as if they were really worth something, but they didn't come in handy units of ten as they do today—we had pounds, shillings and pence. Twelve pennies made a shilling, twenty shillings made a pound, which also amounted to 240 pence, but we also had lots of different denominations of coins and notes.

'Coppers' were what we called all the bronze-coloured small-denomination coins. We had farthings, four to the penny, which were nice little coins with a wren on the back, that ceased to be legal tender in 1960. Ha'pennies, short for halfpennies, two to the penny, had a sailing ship, said to be Sir Francis Drake's Golden Hind, on the back and ceased to be legal tender in 1969. Pennies showed on the back Britannia sitting clutching her trident. On the front (obverse) would be a head and shoulders image of the king or queen who was on the throne when the coin was minted, and each coin also carried the date for that year, which was handy for schoolboy coin collectors wanting to build up a set. (It was one of the things you did, like trainspotting and stamp collecting.) There was also the threepenny piece (known as a thrup'ny bit), which was small, thick and hexagonal, in a brighter shade of bronze—new ones looked as though they were minted of gold. On the reverse of this coin was a thrift plant—probably a hint for potential savers. The more valuable coins were 'silver', but thicker and heavier than today's silver coins. A sixpence was about the size of today's 1p piece. This was the coin that was traditionally put into the Christmas pudding, for children to find, but in cost-conscious households a threepenny piece was often used instead—it could still jam in your windpipe or chip a molar if you met it unexpectedly. A shilling

171

(12 pence) was the same size as today's 5p piece. A florin was two shillings (24 pence) and roughly the same size as today's 10p piece, while half a crown was a size larger still and worth two shillings and six pence (or as we'd have said at the time two-and-six). That was well worth having.

From there on up you had paper notes: the ten shilling, which was a handsome rich chestnut-brown shade and about the size of today's fiver, the slightly larger one-pound note and the far bigger five-pound note, which few people ever saw. Well, most working people didn't earn that much in a whole week. To make things more confusing, some types of transactions were made in guineas. A guinea was one pound and one shilling. The real guinea had become defunct way back in history, so there was no guinea note or coin. But if you'd been buying a racehorse or a valuable piece of art or antique furniture, you'd have been quoted a price in guineas, and the classy association meant that any manufacturer of something a bit expensive priced it in guineas, to make it sound more up-market—it also made it sound cheaper since 50 guineas was in reality fifty pounds and fifty shillings—or putting it another way (with 20 shillings to the pound) £52 10s 0d. It all took a bit of getting to grips with.

But that all changed on the night of 15 February 1971, or D-Day as it was called, when we changed over to today's Continental-style decimal coinage. Despite months of advance preparation, with the government issuing advice about what the new coins looked like and what they were worth (and explaining that for some time we'd have both the old and new coins in our pockets so we'd just have to learn that our old sixpence was now two-and-a-half new pence, our old shilling was 5p, and the florin, 10p), there was carnage. It took twice as long as usual for assistants to work out the change in shops. People also had a good deal of suspicion that prices were being rounded up, to fit the new pricing structure. It all became a bit easier as the old coins were withdrawn, but for many years people held a soft spot for their old thrup'ny bits and farthings, and kept them hoarded in pickle jars stashed away at the backs of cupboards and drawers for sentimental value. And it took years for people to stop converting 'new money' back to 'old' in order to see the real value of whatever it was they were buying—'what, half a crown for that?' made far more sense to most people than 'what, twelve-and-a-half new pence?'

The rise of supermarkets

The first supermarkets came as quite a culture shock. I suppose the idea came over from the United States, as so many modern advances did at the time. But we didn't switch over from small shops to giant supermarkets in one big jump.

First came a semi-traditional type of store with several departments—each of which was like a small specialist counter (fishmongers, butchers, greengrocery and grocers)—grouped under one roof in a shop several times larger than usual; it was a bit like Harrod's Food Hall but nowhere like so posh. International Stores, David Greig and the Home and Colonial Stores were among the first, all now long gone. By patronizing one of these, a busy housewife could cut her daily shopping down to one visit, even though she'd still have to stand in line at each department in turn for the usual service. But—a great innovation, this—instead of paying the shop assistant as usual, these stores had a cashier sitting in a little glass booth at the back, and each shop assistant took your money, popped it into a thing like a cocoa tin, shut the lid and sent it winging its way across the ceiling on a delightful Heath Robinson system of taut wires by pulling a little handle, rather like flushing the loo, to send it on its way. Seconds later, your change would be sent back across the store in the same way. It was riveting to watch and enlivened many a shopping trip for bored small boys. The larger department stores in Leeds and Bradford had a similar system which operated via snaking vacuum tubes and suction, shooting your bill and your money from the counter to accounts on another floor.

There was also the Co-op, which was well known for encouraging regular shoppers long before the days of loyalty cards, by inviting you to become a member. If you joined you would qualify for a 'divi', or dividend, which meant you'd get a few pence knocked off your bill or you could save it up till the end of the year and use it to offset the cost of Christmas.

The first 'real' supermarkets, where you helped yourself using a basket or trolley from loaded aisles of shelves and then paid all in one go at a till, didn't appear in any numbers until the 1960s, though a very few were scattered around the country in the 1950s. (Housewives were a tad apprehensive of them at first; it didn't feel 'right' to be picking up goods and putting them into your basket when you hadn't paid for them, and they missed the chat with the shop assistants.) Early supermarkets were small and sited in town centres, where housewives were already doing their daily shopping. Half the fun of watching reruns of old TV series, such as *The Sweeney*, is seeing Tesco's windows plastered with posters advertising tins of baked beans for 11½d—that's old pence—which in today's money is a tad under 5p. The sight of so many consumer goods piled high and sold cheap, plus the novel opportunity to do all the family shopping under one roof accompanied by light background music (which was introduced to put shoppers in a free-spending mood), proved steadily more irresistible. But it wasn't until the late 1970s that we started to see the first giant out-of-town hypermarkets, as they were known at the time, because it wasn't till then that housewives had their own small cars to go out shopping in.

But the arrival of supermarkets inevitably changed the face of traditional high streets; many small food shops went out of business, and as living standards rose people started shopping for other things than food, especially high-fashion clothes and luxuries unheard of in my youth. Window-shopping became fun, and people bought goods they wanted rather than actually needed. Necessity was no longer the mother of invention; that was a role handed on to people who would become known as 'geeks' and 'nerds'.

Consumer goods

Marketing and advertising—two more new American innovations to reach us—were in their infancy. Everything from groceries to cigarettes originally came in very basic packaging that didn't change for years (and often it had not been altered since wartime 'utility' packaging—using the absolute minimum of wrapping and decoration so as not to waste paper, tin or cardboard). But as the economy improved, everyday goods were gradually given smart new looks, old favourites were improved, and new brand names came onto the market. It was no longer enough for a label to tell you what was inside the tin or packet; a combination of catchy advertisements and attractive packaging was designed to encourage you to try something new.

Cerebos salt came in blue tins with a child pouring salt on a scurrying chick on the front. Gibb's Dentifrice was toothpaste that came in a solid block that you had to scrub away at with a wet toothbrush. Whole families pitched in to the same block with gusto. Brylcreem, made famous by handsome cricketing hero Denis Compton, was a white sticky goo that came in a clear glass jar and was used to slick men's hair down. But as a small boy I was far more concerned with the inner child. I can remember consuming a good deal of Vimto— orangey coloured lemonade—on holidays, and a lot of kids adored Dandelion & Burdock, a rather earthy-tasting fizzy drink, Cream Soda and the highly coloured Cherryade. If you weren't very well, you'd be given Lucozade, which was meant to be a mild tonic that you could have without seeing the doctor, but most of us saw it as a welcome treat in the days when fizzy soft drinks were occasional delights.

Sweetshops were the proper old-fashioned sort. I was very fond of Spangles—square fruit-flavoured boiled sweets which came in colourful paper tubes—though sweetshops were piled high with glass jars of loose sweets. You'd see all the old faithfuls such as aniseed balls, chocolate buttons, gobstoppers, humbugs, dolly mixtures, sherbet lemons, chocolate éclairs and liquorice sticks, which were weighed out into paper bags. You'd have a quarter (4oz, a quarter of a pound) if granny was buying, or an ounce if you were using your own precious pocket money. Sherbet came in cardboard tubes with a stick of liquorice that you licked then dipped in to get the powder out, and penny chews were sold individually. Smaller ones like Black Jacks and Fruit Salad were four-a-penny. Chocolate came in bars of various sizes from the smallest, more like thin, flat, foil-wrapped fingers, selling for a penny or tuppence, up to bars that are more like the ones you see today. We also bought Wagon Wheels—huge round chocolate-covered biscuits that were almost more than even the most devoted choccy-biccy addict could wolf down at a sitting, but we'd make the effort. (The size gradually shrank over the years, I noticed.)

Newsagents had a confectionery counter, too, though a connoisseur would have found the range distinctly lacking compared to that on offer in a proper sweetshop, and they also sold a lot of stuff for smokers that's rarely, if ever, seen nowadays. Cigarettes were largely the sort without filter tips. (Smokers claimed that smoking filter tips was like drinking tea through a sock.) There were Woodbines—cheap and cheerful—Player's Weights, Player's Navy Cut, Capstan Full Strength and Senior Service with their manly outdoor action-man overtones. Ladies would prefer Peter Stuyvesant, and the upper classes would have smart orange-and-silver-coloured boxes of du Maurier, pale-green Balkan Sobranie or Olivier lying around on their Pembroke tables (low coffee tables had not yet been invented).

For pipe smokers there was Condor pipe tobacco and Wills Gold Flake. Proper tobacconists also sold all sorts of exotic pipe tobacco loose in jars, for enthusiasts to 'rub' from a wad of compressed, processed leaves into smokable slivers for themselves. Tobacco was originally promoted as health-giving, and in the 1950s nobody worried that it might not be terribly good for you. Most adults smoked, although the elegant ladies shown in adverts tended to use long, slim cigarette holders. This was thought to look more ladylike than holding a gasper between your knuckles to take a puff, though I never knew anyone in real life who ever used one. And although nobody actually suggested that kids would eventually take up smoking, at Christmas a lot of children would find a packet of sweet cigarettes in the toe of their Christmas stocking—they were sweet white sugary tubes with cherry red ends that tasted rather like dolly mixtures. The other favourite Christmas stocking filler was a sugar mouse—a solid block of vaguely rodent-shaped solidified sugar in pink or white, with a tail made of real old-fashioned string—the same sort that butchers use to truss up the Sunday joint. Sugar mice are still available at a few old-fashioned sweetshops today, but they've long since lost their string tails thanks to modern EC health-and-safety regulations. There is no record, to my knowledge, of anyone ever choking on the tail of a sugar mouse.

Shoe shops were a regular feature of the 'going

back to school' routine. Clarks shoes were well known for being fitted to take care of growing feet, and the highlight of a visit to their shops for us as children was the large high-tech X-ray machine that sat in the centre. You stepped up onto a narrow plinth and slotted your feet into the gap, then through the green screen you could see the outline of your shoes with the skeleton of your feet inside, so that the assistant and your mother could check to see that they were a good fit—in other words, that there was plenty of room for your feet to grow. Nobody wanted to waste good money buying expensive shoes if you were going to grow out of them before the end of term. The X-ray machines didn't stay put for long. I can only assume they were thrown out when the assistants all started glowing in the dark.

By the time I was a teenager, one of the highlights of a Saturday trip into town was a visit to the record shop. There were no racks to browse—you had to know what you wanted, ask the assistant for it, and it would be handed to you over the counter. Pop music had just emerged, and that's what the kids went for. Singles had one song on each side: the famous one that you'd heard on the radio or TV was on the A side and on the back—the B side—was a song that you'd never heard of and rarely played, which I always thought was just there to give value for money. Singles had to be played at the 45rpm setting on your record player, which meant 45 revolutions per minute. There were also EPs which stood for extended play; these carried two songs on each side, and cost correspondingly more. Biggest of all were the dinner-plate-sized LPs—long players, which would have maybe ten or a dozen songs on each side and might contain several hits as well as what you might call second best. To play these, you had to readjust the setting on your record player to a slower speed of 33rpm—if you forgot, the machine played them far too fast so they'd sound like Pinky and Perky on helium.

But since records represented a hefty investment for teenagers with pocket money or young people with their first jobs, you didn't breeze in and buy them, just like that. No, you'd listen to them first. Record shops allocated a lot of space to a row of pegboard booths; you'd go inside, shut the door and the assistant would put the record on a player under the counter, from where the sound was piped into your cubicle. A kid with nothing better to do with their time could spend all Saturday afternoon listening to pop music without buying anything. There were lots of them who liked to hang around town with friends listening to the new releases, window shopping or visiting the coffee bar.

Fashion

As a boy I was never remotely interested in fashion—at least, not until my teens when the ability to attract girls seemed more important than even gardening—but my sister was and so was Mum. Even to me it was obvious that everyone dressed up for special occasions, which in those days included things like travelling by train, going out, visiting relatives, going to church or going out for a walk on Sunday. Most people only owned one or two sets of best clothes, often known as 'Sunday Best' since they were only worn on the day you didn't do everyday jobs that risked messing them up. Once it looked a tad worn, Sunday best would be downgraded to everyday use till it wore out, and you'd have a new set of clothes to be kept 'for best'. Children's clothes usually arrived on the family second-hand grapevine, from older cousins who'd outgrown them.

Grown-ups always wore hats for going out. Ladies did so because it was fashionable; they'd sport a 'turban' (a close-fitting little fabric job) or perhaps a jaunty little number with a scrap of veil over the eyes, looking suspiciously like the black netting gardeners used to keep birds off their strawberries. Ladies' hats had to be firmly secured with hatpins to keep them on, regardless of whether it was windy or not, and to complete the look hats were usually worn with matching gloves. Ladies kept their hats and gloves on in cafés, the cinema and shops—it was only when they arrived back home that they took them off. Gents also wore hats, because a hat spoke volumes about your social status—flat caps were for coalmen and anyone who worked with their hands (though a smart tweed flat cap was high class motoring or motor-cycling attire). Dad had the one he wore for work and a smarter one for Sundays. Bowlers were for city gents, bank managers and middle management, and the slightly less formal Homburgs for others or off-duty wear. Top hats were for toffs out for a day's racing at Royal Ascot or for occasions like smart weddings.

But the great reason for gents wearing hats was because a gentleman always raised his hat if he passed a lady he knew, however slightly, in the street; it was just good manners. A gent also raised his hat for a hearse and kept it held in one hand pressed respectfully to his chest till the cortége had passed. And, of course, they'd always take their hat off before going indoors. (Youths wearing baseball caps indoors still make me uneasy.) Hat racks were standard household kit, kept by the front door and in offices, doctors' surgeries and similar places. They were usually combined with umbrella stands—hooks above and brolly bays, complete with drip trays, below. Most people just had the free-standing sort that could be moved around, but posh houses with a big entrance hall or lobby would have a more sophisticated model that fitted flush to the wall and incorporated a mirror and shelf for pot plants, post and keys.

Women who stayed at home to be full-time housewives and mothers generally wore floral print dresses (often home-made) and sensible flat shoes with peep-toes for 'everyday'; when doing housework they'd put a shoulder-to-knee-length wrap-around pinafore or 'pinnie' over the top to keep their clothes clean. Well, it made sense. Laundry was a much more major job than today, and because most people only owned a few changes of clothes they didn't want to wear them out by washing them more than was absolutely necessary. Since hairstyles were quite elaborate—everyone wanted to look like the film stars they saw at the cinema—most women rolled their hair up in curlers overnight, or they'd put them in during the day but hide them under a headscarf. And they'd always cover their hair when doing housework, to stop it getting dusty or messed up.

But for 'best', women liked to push the boat out a bit. Stiletto-heeled shoes, fur wraps and fancy

*Flared skirts
were all the rage
for the ladies.*

*When it came to looking
smart, there was only
one option—a suit.*

frocks with widely flared skirts were the order of the day. After years of rationing during the war, a woman wanted to look and feel glamorous, and full skirts, frothy petticoats and frocks packed with lots of elaborate detail that took up a good deal of material were the best way she knew of celebrating the return to better times. Trousers were not something women wore. Mother's first pair were a cause célèbre. Since she felt a touch self-conscious about wearing them, she wore them on holiday first, to get used to the idea outside her usual social circle. We were all quite shocked, but secretly I think rather proud that she'd had the nerve.

Young people dressed like their parents when I was a child. We all had the same haircuts—short back and sides for lads, and bobs with side partings for girls. Up to the age of 13 or so I always wore shorts and a shirt, to which I'd add a jumper in winter. You didn't go into long trousers in those days till the fourth form at senior school—they were a badge of seniority, and you wouldn't have dared wear them before you were entitled, however cold the weather. My sister wore pleated skirts, a plain blouse and ankle socks. Older girls wore twinsets, full skirts and stockings—there were no tights at the time. For parties little boys wore suits and little girls wore very full skirts stuck out by layers of frothy stiff petticoats. Glam, eh?

It wasn't until teenagers were invented in the United States and spread here via films, TV and music that young people started to have fashion clothes that let them really express themselves. There were several different looks. There were Teddy boys, with their long, pointed winkle-picker shoes, tight drainpipe trousers, long jackets called 'drapes' with velvet cuffs (based on Edwardian frock coats), topped with a great quiff of hair slicked back with Brylcreem with a cantilevered quiff at the front, just like Elvis, and the sides combed back till they met at the nape of the neck and were glued down with more Brylcreem into a DA (or 'duck's arse'). They'd strut down the high street as if they were the bee's knees, even if their feet were killing them. There were beatniks, with their big baggy sweaters known as 'sloppy Joes' worn above leggings for girls or denim jeans for boys. Beehive hairdos came and went rather quickly since, by all accounts, girls found them the very devil to deal with, what with hours of back-combing and cans of hair spray to glue them in place. When London started swinging, in the early 1960s, lads liked to dress like The Beatles, with shaggy hairdos and fringes you couldn't see out through, and although their collarless suits looked a bit weird, mothers were generally quite relieved that, for a while at least, their sons looked a good deal smarter—and cleaner—than usual. To complete the look, young chaps practised their Liverpudlian phrases—anything that was fashionable was 'gear', not 'cool', the rather old-fashioned phrase that had preceded it. Funny how things come round again.

Then came mods and rockers. Mods were the fashion-conscious ones. The uniform for girls was an eye-opener for us chaps: the very briefest of miniskirts, skimpy tops and long 'kinky boots', often in white patent leather, with short Mary Quant-inspired bobs and a ton of make-up, consisting of white lips and very black eyes with fake eyelashes that made girls look like pandas. For blokes the fashion was for floral shirts and wide 'kipper' ties, not to mention the widest flared trousers the fashion world has ever seen. Rockers were the rough ones who wore motor-biking gear full time, all leather jackets with painted mottoes and crests, crash helmets with cows' horns on top, mean expressions, jeans and oilstains—they were also known as 'greasers' with good reason. Mods and rockers didn't hit it off, as seen on the TV news most summer nights when they met to do battle on the beaches of various popular seaside towns. Brighton was hit particularly badly in the summer of 1964.

Then everyone wanted to be hippies, inspired by the summer of love—1967. The 'uniform' changed to beads, bells and kaftans in psychedelic patterns, with the regulation hairdo of long, straggly hair for girls and long, straggly hair for blokes, backed up by outlandish facial hair. Instead of fighting on the beaches, peace, love and pop festivals became the things to do; Jimi Hendrix and Procul Harum were the rock stars to listen to—and if you could learn yoga and play the sitar so much the better. Even The Beatles were into meditation, under the guidance of Maharishi Mahesh Yogi. Ah, happy, hippy days!

CHAPTER 8

THE WAY WE WERE IN EVERYDAY LIFE

There is always the risk that in hankering for the way things were in the past, you can come over as a malcontent or a misanthrope. But it is hard not to yearn for the way things were when it comes to family life. Today's insularity—fostered to a great extent by the ability to communicate more readily without being face to face—has bred a degree of independence that borders on the antisocial. Most families do not eat together, let alone possess a dining table. Others rely on 'ping meals'. Ping meals? I had to enquire myself on first hearing: microwave meals that are ready when the cooker pings.

We have long acknowledged the wisdom of the phrase 'you can choose your friends but you can't choose your family', and yet it seems to me that there was a greater tolerance back then of familial shortcomings. In the 1950s families were the cornerstone of everyday life, and they were—almost without exception—close in every sense of the word. Most families lived within easy visiting distance of at least some close relatives, so children had a network of cousins to play with, and grandmas and aunts coming round for tea or stepping in for a spot of childcare. And at home mums, dads and kids *did things together*—whether it was days out at weekends or just quiet evenings in. There was only one wireless, maybe a record player and, for the fortunate, a television

187

set. Children would be expected to tidy their own rooms, put away toys and help with a few household chores. Most mothers stayed at home to look after children and take care of the cooking and domestic stuff, and the father was the breadwinner and the acknowledged boss, whose word was law. Well, that's what Mum *said*. Stereotypical though it might sound, an Englishman's home was his castle—he might have to kowtow to the boss at work but at home Jack was his own master.

A sense of responsibility

Family values varied even then, of course. They always have. But most 'nice and normal' families of whatever class were brought up to have a sense of responsibility, and the family came first on our list of priorities. It was taken for granted that 'the family' would care for elderly parents. It wasn't always comfortable, and at times it was a real pain, but it was done out of a sense of duty and 'what was right'. It was very common to find a maiden aunt living in the home of a relative or for nearby grannies and great-aunts to have a standing invitation to spend Sundays with the family and stay for lunch and tea. Grandma Titch and Auntie Alice (my father's mother and sister) were typical of that particular breed of mother and spinster daughter who lived together uncomfortably all their lives. At Christmas and Easter, even tiny family houses would be bursting at the seams with relatives. And a newly-wed son or daughter would nearly always live at home with one or other of their parents for the first few weeks, months or years of married life while they saved up for a place of their own.

Our mum worked at Lister's Mill in nearby Addingham from the day she left school at 14 until she was married. Once a family came along most mothers didn't go out to work but looked after the children; they'd read them bedtime stories— everything from old favourites such as *Red Riding Hood* to Beatrix Potter's tales of Peter Rabbit, Jemima Puddleduck and Squirrel Nutkin, Enid Blyton's Noddy stories and—in London and for the middle classes—*Winnie the Pooh*. And they'd sing nursery rhymes, walk their children to and from school until they were big enough to go on their own, make tea when they came home, and then help them with their reading.

Being a full-time mum was no easy task since everything had to be done by hand. Modern supermarkets hadn't appeared and there were few convenience foods, electrical appliances or labour-saving gadgets to help with household chores. Mothers knitted and sewed, they cooked proper meals from scratch and went out shopping for fresh food almost every day. Since there was more than a flavour of postwar austerity, mothers were naturally thrifty, so everything was used up and nothing went to waste. And they didn't complain. The attitude that prevailed in the 1950s was: 'Get on with it and stop making a fuss.' Saints? Not at all; just folk who knew what they had to do and who got on with it— with the occasional grumble, of course—they were still human—but they had a capacity for grinning and bearing it that is still buried deep within us should we care to use it.

People didn't rely on the state to solve their problems or see them through. Oh, they might still have talked about 'them' and 'us', but it was to the family they turned in times of trouble, and you could always rely on friends and neighbours for assistance in all sorts of ways. In those days you knew who they were, for two reasons—first, folk did not move house as frequently as they do nowadays and, second, people were rather more outgoing and lacked the insularity that is all-pervasive today.

It would be wrong to suggest that everyone was the same, especially when it came to the way they used their money. Some would spend the entire contents of their wage packet by the following Friday, would live in rented accommodation and buy things on tick or the never-never. Hire purchase was the smart term, but it was not a system favoured by a lot of folk. Most were—to use the word of a recent Prime Minister—prudent. Not that they used that word. They would say—in the case of my mum—that they were saving for a rainy day. (Though I did wonder if she would ever notice when it was pouring down.) Mums would join Christmas clubs where you paid in so much each week and collected enough by December to pay for your turkey and all the trimmings. Or they might treat themselves, just occasionally, to something that was needed, such as an electric kettle or new iron, from Mrs So-and-so's catalogue—it could be paid off in just a year with weekly instalments. That was the nearest my mum got to the never-never. She was rather disapproving of one lady over the road who smoked (in itself not to be encouraged in women) and who bought her children a new bike at Christmas thanks to saving up Kensitas gift tokens. When American Express—many years later—coined the expression 'Frees you from pre-set spending limits', my mother asked: 'Doesn't that

LOCAL LIVING

Most people didn't travel far for work, school, entertainment or shopping. Everything you needed was on the doorstep. Housewives shopped daily for bread, meat and such veg as they didn't grow for themselves, and virtually everything on their shopping list was either made, grown or reared locally so there was little in the way of long-distance road transport and few heavy trucks or delivery vans to jam the streets.

Apart from petrol for the occasional car, even small communities were almost self-sufficient. Every small town or village was rather like your extended family, with their own personalities and sense of identity. Every community had its own cricket team. Lads thought it an honour to be selected, and they'd turn out on summer weekends to play neighbouring teams. Everyone who could supported local activities from the Women's Institute, Boy Scouts and Girl Guides, to church socials and choir or bell ringing; well, they were the roots of your social life. And in those days you did mix with other people instead of spending time alone in your room at home with an electronic gadget for company; even if the technology had existed you'd have been thought rather unsociable if you shut yourself away for more than an hour or so. You could find everything you needed for everyday life and have a good time without travelling far from home or spending much money.

mean "allows you to live beyond your means?"'

We had good role models when I was a nipper. People in the public eye were—for the most part—respected and respectable; apart from those who blotted their copybook. And there were a few. But in most cases they at least had the decency to evince some kind of embarrassment or contrition. The people we looked up to were sportsmen, dignitaries from the mayor (usually, though sometimes he could be a bit 'above himself') to the prime minister, and, of course, the royal family. Edward VIII had blotted *his* copybook in no uncertain terms with Mrs Simpson but that was now forgotten since we had at least 'ended up with the right man' in the shape of his brother, King George VI. Famous singers, actors and film stars led very different lives from ours, but nobody was much interested in their private affairs—we kept them on the pedestals where they belonged, since we wanted to believe that the men really were suave and the women pure and glamorous. In any case, it was not a good career move for politicians, singers or film stars to be involved in scandals—the outcome of bad behaviour was a swift fall from grace, and usually meant losing their job.

The media tended to cover far more good-news stories, and anything about great British achievements was always top of the bill. The ones that especially stand out from my childhood were the Coronation, the conquest of Everest and Donald Campbell breaking various speed records before his untimely death on Coniston Water. Murders, divorces, vandalism or civil disobedience were certainly reported, but, apart from the odd outrage such as the Rillington Place murders by

John Christie, they were not the sort of thing *nice people* wanted to know about on a daily basis.

Manners, etiquette and keeping up appearances

Good manners and respect for your elders and betters were the glue that stuck society together. Old people and pillars of society were valued, and gents behaved in a chivalrous manner towards ladies, always holding doors open for them (and they were called ladies then, not 'women', which at the time suggested a rather older and lower-class lady). If a man was seated at a table, he stood up when a lady joined him, and all the men present would stand up if a lady visitor came into the room. Gents raised their hats—or at least doffed their caps—to women they knew, however slightly, and a man would always walk on the outside of the pavement—the idea being that he'd shelter the woman from having her clothes splashed if a car went through a puddle as they walked along together. Now I have to tell you that having been brought up to do all this in my youth and childhood I still do it today. Many men do. But there will be those who think that a lot of it seems positively non-PC now, especially when you hear of blokes being sent off on re-education courses when they've been 'reported' for some sexist sin such as opening a door to a lady (sorry, woman).

Even the dead were shown deep respect in the early part of the twentieth century. Men took their hats off and held them closely to their chest when a hearse went by, and when someone died the curtains were kept drawn in their house, and at one time the whole street would follow suit. Newly widowed women wore black for a while after the funeral, even though it wasn't still measured strictly as it had been in Victorian times, but some very old ladies nevertheless wore black full time. I was never sure if it was a uniform or just a habit.

A lot of manners came into everyday family life. They were ingrained into us from early on. We were all brought up to say 'please' and 'thank you', and to be punctual. Table manners were very rigid. You sat down in your rightful place, and father naturally sat at the head of the table, with mother opposite him. Some families said grace before every single meal, but certainly you'd expect it on special occasions like Christmas and often before Sunday lunch. Even when grace was over you didn't wade in; you waited until everyone had been served before starting to eat. You were expected to use your knife and fork properly and to chew everything thoroughly; bolting your food was quite out of order as was eating with your mouth open. During a meal you'd make polite conversation, but there'd be no speaking with your mouth full. If the family had visitors even better manners than usual were expected, and if there was any doubt that there might not be quite enough food to go round, one parent—usually the mother— would murmur under her breath 'FHB'—short for 'family hold back'—so that guests didn't go short. And if you were the first to finish your meal, you sat politely until everyone else finished too—there was no getting down and rushing off to play until you'd been given permission to get down from the table.

If you went to other people's houses, you were automatically on your very best behaviour. On visits with your mother, you sat politely, however bored

194

you might be by the adult conversation, without fidgeting or interrupting. You certainly didn't rush off and turn on their TV or explore the house for something to play with. It just wasn't done, and your mother would have been terribly embarrassed to be let down by her children's bad behaviour. And you'd know all about it when you got back home. God, it was boring! But you did it.

Punishment for lapses in manners or bad behaviour generally would have been anything from being sent to your room without supper, loss of outings or some anticipated treat, to a good talking to from your dad, which might possibly be followed by an uncomfortable few minutes with 'the slipper' or—in our case—a whalebone hairbrush. It was only used as a last resort, but most of the time the mere threat was enough.

The only people, strangely enough, who were allowed a shocking breach of table manners were grandfathers. They'd pour their tea into their saucer and blow on it to cool it, and then drink it straight out of the saucer. Mine always did, and so it seems did a lot of other people's grandads. We were certainly never allowed to do so. I knew better than to try. It seemed like a privilege that went with age and status in the family. But I hoped that when I was as old as him, I'd earn the right to drink my tea out of a saucer too. I haven't started yet. Well, a chap must have something to look forward to.

As a child, life was dotted with little homilies that were trotted out at any opportunity as an instant reminder of what was expected of you. 'If you can't say anything nice, don't say anything at all', 'children should be seen and not heard', 'now, now, that'll do', or if all else failed there'd be the rather more to the point 'don't show off'. Schoolchildren were taught the correct way to cross the road—look right, left, then right again, and if the road is clear 'quick march'—don't run. We were told not to talk to strangers and to keep our school cap on until we reached home and changed out of our school uniform. Oh, there were so many things to remember.

Homes and furnishings

When Mum and Dad bought their first home—a three-storey Victorian terraced cottage, number 34 Nelson Road, Ilkley—they paid £400 for it, on a mortgage, in the autumn of 1949. It was an enormous expense at the time. Buying your own house was quite a feather in any family's cap since at the time most working people only ever lived in rented accommodation. But it felt like a terrible risk. People wondered if they'd ever get their money back if they wanted to sell at some time in the future.

Our house was much the same as most people had when I was small: two up and two down and an attic. It had a back kitchen and a 'front room' (as the sitting room was known) but no porch or entrance hall—you just walked straight into the front room, and under the floor was the coal cellar, which was filled via a chute from the coal-hole outside in the garden. Upstairs was the loo and two bedrooms, a double for Mum and Dad and a single for me, with an attic overhead. We moved in a while after I was born. Until then we'd lived at Grandma Titch's house, which was just round the corner, a ten-minute walk away. When my sister

Kath came along Dad divided up the attic, turning half the space into a bedroom for me and the rest into a bathroom. We were lucky to have one—lots of people still managed without. Grandma Titch *never* had an indoor loo or bathroom, and she only died in the 1970s, aged over 80. She and Auntie Alice, who lived with her, made do with a pot under the bed, a tin bath in front of the fire once a week, and a 'strip wash' with a sponge or face-flannel at a basin in their bedrooms between times. Mind you, as soon as we had a bathroom put in they got into the habit of dropping round once a week to use ours.

Accommodation for most people was a bit basic, but you didn't mind because in those days no one had a very high standard of living, and interior design had never been heard of for the working classes. Families ate at a table and chairs in the kitchen for everyday meals, and there were no fitted kitchens. You had a sink, maybe a freestanding wooden 'cabinet' with glazed doors and a drop-down front, and a larder for storing food. Mind you, my dad did make a 'breakfast bar' in the late 1950s. It had a drop-down flap and stools that we could sit on. It was what my mother called 'contemporary'. If the lady of the house wanted to make pastry, decorate a cake or stuff the Christmas turkey, she'd stand at the kitchen table—or in Mum's case her new 'worktop'—to do it. If houses had a separate dining room at all it was kept for special occasions so that the best china, serviettes and bone-handled cutlery didn't get worn out. Well, you had to keep something in reserve to impress visitors or to bring out at Christmas.

Ordinary families didn't own lots of stuff that

had to be put away, so you didn't need a lot of cupboards. Bedrooms had a small free-standing wardrobe and a chest of drawers, which was quite enough when you didn't own many clothes. Living rooms were just that, the room the whole family spent most of their time in. Furnishings were sparse. You had rugs on floorboards or maybe a square of carpet with bare boards showing round the edge, but not wall-to-wall carpets. If the boards were not in very good condition, they would be given a coat of dark-brown stain. Most families had a couple of armchairs and a sofa round the fireplace, and a small cottage upright piano was essential—it was as much a status symbol as anything. A few people had pianolas, which were pianos that played themselves when you inserted a roll bearing what looked like Braille into its innards and pumped away at two pedals with your feet— they were fascinating, even if a bit of a cheat.

When couples moved into their first home, their furniture usually came from relatives because few of them could afford to buy new until quite well into their domestic life. A lot of families only ever had second-hand stuff from a saleroom or inherited bits and pieces. People were glad for anything they could get. At home Mum had a bit of a thing for sitting-room furniture; she grew bored with it quickly, so we were always taking one lot down to the saleroom and bringing back something else. But we were unusual; most people kept the same furniture for decades and only replaced it when it fell apart.

There were very few electrical gadgets because most of the ones we take for granted today simply didn't exist. You'd have a large wireless set with

198

valves that took a few minutes to warm up in the living room, but no TV in the early 1950s. Some people still had wind-up gramophones, with a tin of needles that you could only use a few times each before they went blunt, that played heavy shellac 78s, which were very brittle and broke easily. But these were soon replaced when a brand-new electric Fidelity or a Dansette record player was bought. We bought ours, a Fidelity with a red leatherette cover, from a neighbour's home-shopping catalogue, and Dad started building up a collection of classical records. Instead of vacuum cleaners, people pushed a Ewbank carpet sweeper round their carpet square in the middle of the living room, and they'd take rugs outside to shake them or drape them over the washing line and bash them with a cane carpet-beater. Electricity was still a bit of a modern innovation, and people of our parents' age could still remember what it was like to get by with just gaslight of an evening.

When people moved house they had to list their electrical appliances for the electricity board as a rough guide to likely consumption. Most rooms only had one single electric socket, plus an overhead light in the centre of the ceiling. In towns and cities kitchens usually had a gas or electric stove, but only a few of the most 'modern' kitchens ran to a fridge. A fifties fridge had a huge cabinet housing lots of electrical gubbins, but only a tiny space inside for food. Ours, when we finally got one, only held two bottles of milk, a block of margarine, which was used as a cheap alternative to butter, and some cheese. Some people's fridges had a slot inside the top of the cabinet for a metal ice-cube maker, but this was reckoned a great luxury. We didn't have one till our original fridge was replaced with a newer model years later. Even when a wider range of electrical kitchen appliances started to come in, they were nowhere like as labour-saving as today's versions.

Home improvements

No sooner had people got their first homes than they started to do them up. They needed a fair bit of modernization, since the nation's housing stock was in a pretty poor state; we hadn't recovered fully from the war. The national census of 1951 revealed that only one house in three had a bath, and one in 20 still had no piped water. There were still large estates of prefabs—the prefabricated bungalows that were thrown up in a hurry to house people who'd been bombed out—which were meant to be temporary but still existed well into the 1960s. Some people bought old railway carriages, put them on vacant land and knocked the interior about a bit to make it habitable. Those at seaside resorts became very popular as cheap holiday homes for decades, before being gradually built onto until they were 'absorbed' into more conventional bungalows.

Being a plumber my dad was pretty good with his hands; he set about gradually turning our Victorian terraced house into a more contemporary home. He converted the attic, installed central heating and a bathroom, put in modern floorboards and doors, replaced the original range with a small fireplace which had mottled cream tiles, then redecorated the whole place. DIY was fast becoming the big new craze. Every father became his own amateur handyman, with *Do It Yourself* magazine and the

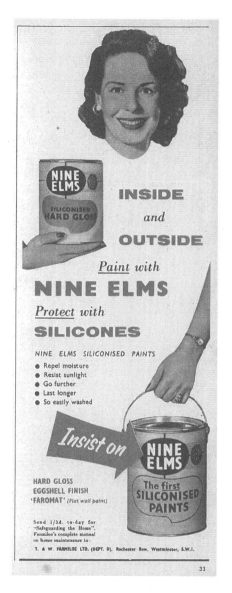

People were proud of their homes. They made sure the insides were spick and span and the gardens neat and tidy.

TV handyman Barry Bucknell showing you how to fix a sheet of hardboard to a panelled Victorian door to make it 'flush' before fitting it with a plastic handle and a ball catch to make it open and close more easily. The first fitted kitchen cabinets and built-in bedroom wardrobes were only just coming in, but what everyone wanted was central heating. The first versions had a solid-fuel boiler that was fuelled by coke, and since it was thought too extravagant (or just plain unnecessary) to heat the bedrooms, people only put in part central heating, which meant your boiler only fed a few downstairs radiators leaving the heat to rise naturally to take the chill off the upstairs rooms. We were one of the first families in our street to have central heating, but that was largely because Dad re-used a boiler he took out at another job. Why spend good money on new when you could have something second-hand for free?

Naturally everyone wanted to make their house look its best, and that meant redecorating in the latest styles. The fashion at the time was for 'busy' wallpaper with floral patterns for bedrooms and a bamboo or rush-like effect for living rooms, with a frieze round the top and a trio of plaster-of-Paris ducks flying in formation up one of the walls. So, it wasn't just Hilda Ogden—we all had 'em. You might also have a painting hanging on the wall—there was one of an Oriental lady with a green face that everyone seemed to have for a while before she went out of fashion. The artist was Tretchikoff, a Russian-born South African. Not that any of us knew or cared at the time. The Green Lady just had this wistful stare. My mum never liked her . . .

As soon as people started to have a little cash

to spare for luxuries, houseplants became a great craze. The wide windowsills of pre-war houses made great natural display spaces, and in most rooms they were the only places plants had enough light. (Mind you, you couldn't risk leaving them on the windowsills on cold winter nights—you had to move them onto a table overnight when you drew the curtains.) Since so few houses still had central heating, the favourite houseplants were the naturally more indestructible kinds: spider plants, money plants, zonal pelargoniums, partridge-breasted aloes and bryophyllums—those strange-looking succulents that produce rows of baby plantlets all round the edges of their leaves. You hardly ever see them nowadays; we'd keep every single 'baby' and pot them up to give away to friends or put on bring-and-buy stalls. About the most exotic thing most people grew were busy Lizzies, which we rooted in jars of water and passed round. Our few houseplants were like old friends, and most people would have a selection in various stages of decrepitude lined up along windowsills till eventually they died or had been so raided for cuttings that they looked like gnarled old stumps. We didn't throw them away till they were well and truly dead.

The garden

Most houses had two gardens, front and back, which both had very different uses. The front was for show and the back was for family.

The front garden was really for the benefit of passers-by and the neighbours. It was to be admired but not touched. It had to be kept looking good, come what may, because otherwise 'what would people think?' Homes with a fair bit of space out the front had a posh lawn—invariably square or rectangular—which was absolutely never to be walked on, with perhaps a bit of neatly clipped privet hedge and a formal flower bed. You might have bedding plants lined up in straight rows, lobelia and alyssum alternately round the edge, orange French marigolds next, then scarlet salvias and a few taller 'dot plants' arranged symmetrically down the middle. Or you could choose rose beds, planted with hybrid teas and floribundas, usually all the same colour. Varieties with patriotic names were especially popular, such as 'Peace' (named to celebrate the end of the War) or 'Queen Elizabeth' (which was strong, upright and very reliable). They'd be kept immaculately—pruned down to stubs every winter, heavily manured every spring, and sprayed regularly against all the regular rose disorders, using a great big brass syringe loaded with chemical jollup from the bucket in which it had been mixed up. The earth beneath them would be bare and weed free—underplanting had not yet been thought of for rose beds.

Needless to say, front garden flowers were not to be picked. Some houses had a bit of a rockery in the front, but don't imagine it was anything remotely natural-looking—the 1950s version consisted of a pile of soil spread over rubble, studded with lumps of stone (or often chunks of concrete) and dotted with low-spreading flowers such as aubretia and snow-in-summer. But even people with very small frontages made an effort. Ours had a tiny patch of lawn with lily of the valley in a narrow border round the edge, backed by a privet hedge. A lot of people with really minuscule front gardens just covered them with gravel to keep their surroundings tidy. There was no decking.

Back gardens were still quite formal—all straight lines and neat edges, but at least as children you were allowed out there to play. Most people had a rectangle of lawn with borders round the edge, planted with a mixture of shrubs and herbaceous flowers, with privet hedges round the boundary. There'd usually be a veg patch down the far end with the shed, and this 'utility area' was often separated from the prettier part of the garden by a screen of rustic poles with climbing and rambler roses growing on it. 'Dorothy Perkins' was everywhere, despite her penchant for mildew. Veg gardens were more like mini-allotments—people didn't grow anything exotic, it was just the basic things that they always used in the kitchen, mostly potatoes, 'greens' and onions.

Somewhere or other most gardens had a fruit tree, which was great for climbing, usually a Bramley apple, some sort of eating apple or a Victoria plum—there were no dwarf rootstocks in those days, so fruit trees reached a fair old size. You needed a ladder to pick the fruit unless you simply waited for it to fall off, which meant it was always bruised and wouldn't keep. An average-sized veg patch usually had a blackcurrant bush or the odd gooseberry, which was used for jam or fruit pies. Any surplus was bottled and brought out to make pies in the winter. The other thing you'd find in a lot of fifties gardens, which seems out of place today, was a tortoise. It might not have been the most exciting companion, but it didn't eat much and it wasn't going to run away. You kept it in a little wire-netting run on the lawn and put it in a box of straw in the shed every winter to hibernate. If you were lucky, it would emerge again the following spring. Many didn't. No wonder tortoises are not available today—you have to go to the zoo to see them, unless you know an old lady or gent who still has their old family pet. But it was all part of what people thought of as a family garden at the time.

Our back garden was nothing of the sort. Father wasn't into gardening. Outside the back of our house was a tiny yard where we kept our bikes, leaning against a wall and covered in a bit of old carpet. They were next to the dustbins, and the bin for the leftover food scraps that a neighbour would collect to feed to his pigs. The only plant life was a flowering currant bush by the back door trimmed into a huge cube by Dad each summer; the leaves released their sharp blackcurranty scent every time someone pushed past it. Beyond the yard ran a narrow lane, 'the back', and our 'proper' back garden was the other side of this.

It still wasn't what you'd call big, only about 30 foot long and 15 foot wide, and most of the space was taken up by a giant sycamore tree that cut out the light. There was a derelict old stone outhouse that I was strictly forbidden from going into, which I always assume had once been the old outside toilet, a rectangle of grass, which you couldn't dignify with the title lawn, and a bit of border that had once grown a few spuds and sprouts but now just held a hydrangea and some indestructible montbretia and 'Esther Read' daisies, with the usual mouldy-looking 'Dorothy Perkins' rose rambling along the rusty wire fence.

206

That was it. Hardly the sort of thing to kick-start a gardening career. But it was a great place to play since you could run around without being shouted at and there was none of that 'keep off the flower beds' business that kids of garden-mad dads had to put up with. And as soon as I started to take a real interest, it's where I cleared my first flower bed and sowed my first packets of seeds. I remember it well; they came up with a great bald footprint in the middle where Dad had stepped by mistake at a crucial stage in their development.

The allotment

Anyone who didn't have enough garden to satisfy their needs took an allotment. Despite the general decline in self-sufficient gardening after the War, virtually every town and city still had its own allotment plots. They were no great objects of beauty; the holders prided themselves on doing everything on the cheap. Well, that was after all the whole point of growing your own—to save money.

Allotment holders cobbled their own greenhouses together from old window frames and made ramshackle sheds out of old floorboards. They used soot collected from their chimneys at home to make little barriers round their crops to protect them from slugs, and soot water was sprayed onto brassicas to deter caterpillars. Oh, it was good stuff, but you can't do it today of course: health and safety . . .

My very first introduction to gardening was via Grandpa's allotment; it was by the River Wharfe, and I can still remember wandering down his rows of sweet peas to the sound of clinking cocoa tin lids that he strung up to frighten off the birds.

Apart from sweet peas, which he grew especially for Grandma, all the available space was packed solid with serious stuff like potatoes, onions, Savoy cabbages and rhubarb. Allotment holders with growing families needed bulk to fill hungry mouths, not a lot of fancy crops that took a lot of time and trouble to grow and then weren't worth the effort. Grandpa also grew blackberries. I remember them particularly since he supported them on old brass bedsteads that today would be worth a small fortune. There were the odd few tomatoes but always in one of the shanty-style greenhouses that were so common at allotments; in the 1950s we were still having hard winters, and even in summer Yorkshire was no place for outdoor tomatoes.

Today allotments have become trendy, with long waiting lists in many areas, and alongside the greens and King Edwards you'll find all sorts of rare and exotic 'designer' veg, cut-flower crops, willows for basketwork, rows of grapes for home-made wine and fruit for making into fashionable smoothies and juices. Long-retired venerable old allotment-hands will be working side by side with doctors, lawyers, middle class mums and young families and wondering whatever happened to the old men in their flat caps.

Grandpa Hardisty on his allotment.

208

Radio and TV

The first real home entertainment for families was a hefty great wireless set (usually known as the 'steam radio') parked in the living room. It had a large cabinet made of thick brown bakelite (or, in posh models, polished walnut), a couple of dials, and a long panel showing all the available stations, which lit up, after a few minutes, when the set was switched on. Originally you could get three BBC stations: the Home Service (news, current affairs and other serious stuff), the Third Programme (classical music) or the Light Programme (light music and entertainment), and any number of exotic-sounding foreign stations such as Luxembourg and Hilversum. We often wondered what was on those. But children weren't allowed to fiddle with the dials, and most of us didn't dare touch them in case we broke something.

A housewife might turn the wireless on during the day for a bit of company while she was doing the housework. *Housewives' Choice* was packed with cheery tunes, and *Mrs Dale's Diary* was probably the first soap opera most people remember, though the term hadn't been invented at the time. *Workers' Playtime* was another popular music selection, meant to enliven the time for people working in factories; it went out three times a week at lunchtime, from a factory canteen 'somewhere in Britain', as it had done during the War, to boost morale. At times when the whole family would be together the schedules were peppered with a variety of comedy programmes: *Hancock's Half Hour*, *The Goon Show*, *Take*

It From Here, *The Clitheroe Kid* (with Jimmy Clitheroe), *The Navy Lark* and *Round the Horne*. Every day brought another dose of *The Archers* which was, at the time, still largely an educational programme for farmers; the scriptwriters diluted serious agricultural advice with the daily doings of a fictional farming family to encourage people to listen in. The most memorable episode was on 22 September 1955, the night Grace Archer died in the fire, which it's thought was deliberately timed to compete with the launch of ITV. One of the very few other radio programmes that have stayed the course is *Gardeners' Question Time*. In those days the team of experts consisted of three elderly gents who spent half their time arguing with each other about the finer points of growing something you'd usually never heard of, but it made irresistible listening. You imagined them all coming to blows round the back afterwards—if they could wait that long.

There were news broadcasts during the day, the 'pips' from Greenwich telling you the time on the hour every hour, and the evening play or various educational programmes which you sat and listened to as a family in the evenings. By the time I was a bit older, there was the *Today* programme which, when I first remember it, was presented by the bumblingly eccentric Jack de Manio. Rather than major news stories punctuated with hard-hitting political interviews, he chose instead to talk to dolphin trainers in Florida or conduct interviews from a hole in the road outside Broadcasting House. His penchant was for offbeat stories. One I particularly remember was about a fire-eater at a circus who hiccuped in the middle

210

WHO'S WHO FROM THE
GOLDEN DAYS
OF RADIO COMEDY

As comedy became a tad more risqué, BBC bosses laid down rules for scriptwriters in 'The Green Book' regarding what was considered acceptable taste and decency. Writers naturally regarded it as a challenge to stretch the rules as far as they could, and so a good deal of radio comedy was packed with double entendres and also poked fun at traditional Establishment figures, which delighted a public who were feeling rather pushed around after years of compulsory military service and wartime rules and regulations. A good many comedians whose careers started on popular radio shows went on to become household names on TV. Here's a little of what we were listening to at the time.

The Glums
The domestic doings of the ghastly Glum family, featured Jimmy Edwards as the oafish and overbearing Pa Glum, Dick Bentley as the idiot son Ron and June Whitfield as Eth, his long-suffering girlfriend. They were a feature on the weekly programme, *Take It From Here*.

'Oh Ron!', 'Oh, Eth,' they would sigh to one another, as we kids raised our eyes to heaven, not really seeing the joke.

The Goon Show

A series of almost surrealistic situations featuring bizarre, but much loved, characters such as Neddie Seagoon, Bluebottle and Minnie Bannister, played by ex-servicemen Harry Secombe, Peter Sellers, Spike Milligan and Michael Bentine; episodes were full of typical rough army banter, a bit rude and disrespectful of authority and 'the Establishment' (some people considered it a bit subversive), with myriad home-made sound effects. One BBC executive was heard to ask 'What is this thing, the Go-on Show?'

Hancock's Half Hour

A series of episodes in the life of a pretentious loser; each episode revolved around a topic such as Tony Hancock's attempt to be a blood donor, a radio ham, a juror or a passenger in a lift that gets stuck between floors. Various events centred on his house, 23 Railway Cuttings, East Cheam, and his rather trying lodgers Bill Kerr, Hattie Jacques and Sid James. It started on the Light Programme in 1956 (now Radio 2), then moved to TV in black and white.

The Navy Lark
Leslie ('Oh, I say!') Phillips, Richard Caldicot (Captain Povey), Jon (ga-ber-ga ber-ga-ber) Pertwee and Heather Chasen (Wren Chasen) in a comedy about the British Navy that aired every Sunday lunchtime. 'Coming into Portsmouth—sideways' became a catchphrase in our household.

Round the Horne
Kenneth Horne, Kenneth Williams and Hugh Paddick in a hugely irreverent, suggestive— and delightfully camp—sketch show which became, and still is, a cult.

of his performance and sent out a jet of flame straight at the pianist who provided his musical accompaniment, setting fire to his sheet music. It was far more fun than listening to a lot of boring old politicians waffling on.

In later years, pirate radio stations came along with their mix of pop records and disc jockeys (such as Simon Dee) broadcasting illegally from a little way offshore. School kids tuned in to Radio Veronica, Radio Atlanta and then Radio Caroline and felt wonderfully naughty crouched beneath the sheets with their 'crystal sets' before transistor radios became the vogue. Then the BBC launched its own youth music channel, Radio 1, and we had a station we could listen to 'officially'. All the other BBC radio stations were given numbers as well, as part of the modernizing process, but there is still a patriotic thrill to be had for those of a certain age when the words 'This is the BBC Home Service' are occasionally hauled out of the archives and broadcast to remind us of old times.

TV added a new dimension to family entertainment. It was a huge novelty. In 1950 there were only 350,000 sets in Britain, and only four people out of every hundred had one. (Just compare that to today, when most homes have several sets, in the living room, bedrooms, study and kitchen, and people can access TV programmes over their home computers and mobile phones.) Dad bought our first TV set in 1958, and we were one of the first houses in our street to have one. Most TV sets at the time were enormous cabinets with a tiny little screen set in the top, but ours was a surprisingly compact Pye with very few knobs— just the basic on/off, volume and tuning knobs at the front, plus brightness, contrast, and vertical and horizontal hold round the back, which Dad twiddled to get a decent picture. It only had one channel: the BBC. All the local kids wanted to come round to watch it with us, until their parents bought sets of their own. It opened up a whole new world, even though broadcasts at first only ran for a few hours every afternoon and evening with close-down at 11pm. Well, the authorities didn't want to keep breadwinners up too late, when they had to be out to work early the next morning.

For small kids there was *Watch with Mother* shortly after lunch. Monday was *Picture Book* (a story with pictures); Tuesday brought *Andy Pandy*, along with his cuddly-toy sidekicks Teddy and Looby Loo; on Wednesday came *The Flowerpot Men*, who talked gobbledegook ('Ah, flob-a-dob') and lived in a garden with their friend Little Weed. Thursdays was always devoted to a rabbit, a hedgehog and a mouse—*Rag, Tag and Bobtail*—and on Fridays we had *The Woodentops*, a puppet family with their pet Spotty Dog. All but *Picture Book* were puppet shows, which we all loved, though parents weren't so sure about Bill and Ben, in case we all started talking the same way as them: 'Wobbot a lobodob of rubbidish'.

Children's TV came back on in the late afternoon with programmes such as *Whirlybirds* which featured the daring exploits of a helicopter and its two dashing pilots Chuck and P.T. I also liked *Popeye* cartoons, with the spinach-eating sailor, his skinny girlfriend Olive Oyl and the bully Bluto, but they were only shown on the new ITV. We just had BBC, so they were a treat to be enjoyed when we visited our cousins, who had a newer set

215

that could get *both* channels. I was also quite keen on cowboys: Range Rider or the Lone Ranger with his horse Silver and Red Indian sidekick Tonto; it was always easy to follow the plot since the goodies were always dressed in light grey or white and rode white horses, while the baddies wore black with horses to match. In case you were left in any doubt about who was who, the Lone Ranger was known for his catchphrase 'Hi-ho Silver; away!', uttered whenever he dashed off at a gallop after the baddies. We also had *Crackerjack*, hosted by Eamonn Andrews, who ran games and handed out *Crackerjack* pencils as consolation prizes; the glove puppets Sooty and Sweep with their 'minder' Harry Corbett; and cartoons featuring the swashbuckling but inept Captain Pugwash. Oh, it was all great fun. At first TV would close down for an hour or so after children's programmes ended leaving only the test card on show, so that mothers could put toddlers to bed without them wanting to stay up and watch TV. But that fell by the wayside after a while.

The evening's grown-up entertainment began with the news which, originally, was read by a very serious chap with an awfully Oxford accent wearing full evening dress, right down to starched shirt and dicky bow. (Lady newsreaders weren't allowed, since the BBC bosses felt they'd be unable to cope with some of the more harrowing stories without breaking down.) *Tonight* with Cliff Michelmore featured a mix of news, current events and entertainment, with a topical calypso sung by the West Indian Cy Grant or a comical song from the comedian Lance Percival. We had the legal series *Perry Mason* starring Raymond Burr as the defence attorney who always won his case, and *Dixon of Dock Green*, the police drama with Jack Warner, which was so popular that Jack continued in the role till well past the age when real policemen were pensioned off. When commercial television started up we were enthralled by the first soap operas, such as *Emergency—Ward 10*, a medical drama, and *Coronation Street*, which, of course, is still with us today.

There was Barry Bucknell, the TV handyman, showing fifties' fathers how to make all the latest must-have home improvements such as a cocktail cabinet. Dad was very dismissive, complaining that 'his panel pins have already been knocked in'—no doubt to save time on air, since all programmes went out 'live', but Dad still thought it was cheating. The weekend schedules were heavy with variety shows, which were made up of a mixture of music and comedy acts; these brought to the fore a lot of all-round entertainers, such as Ken Dodd, Bruce Forsyth, Eric Morecambe and Ernie Wise, who'd started out as song-and-dance men in music halls and small provincial theatres.

The *Billy Cotton Band Show* was a regular, featuring the delightful black pianist Winifred Atwell along with male counterparts such as Joe 'Mr Piano' Henderson and Russ Conway, who the ladies loved for his habit of cheekily winking at the camera during his performances—his best known tune was 'Side Saddle'. The winsome Scottish singer Kathy Kay sang wistful ballads, to be followed by the rather more glamorously lip-glossed Kathy Kirby who would belt out 'Secret Love'. Liberace (Lee to his friends) was another great favourite with the ladies, with his sparkly suits, big smile and curly blonde bouffant hairdo. 'Such a nice boy,' they'd say, 'American of course.' They'd also have the trumpet-player George Chisholm making a cheery racket with his jazz band or guest artistes such as The Temperance Seven (famous for 'Pasadena'). Another regular favourite was *The Black and White Minstrel Show* (dropped rather quickly once TV became PC), and a bit later came *Sunday Night at the London Palladium*, hosted by a succession of famous names, not least Bruce Forsyth. It must have made a great impression on kids at the time, since a lot of us were allowed to stay up to see it till the very end—including the competition 'Beat the Clock'—before being sent up to bed.

Some programmes, however, seemed more designed to send kids screaming to bed or at least hiding behind the settee, because the Big New Thing was science fiction. At the time sputniks were very much in the news and the space race was in its infancy, so 'things from outer space' were very much on people's minds. 'Were there such things as Martians,' we all wondered, 'and if so, what were they like—and would they come here?' We rather hoped so, if only so we could see if they were really little green men with pointy heads and antennae instead of ears. The early TV sci-fi series such as *The Quatermass Experiment* (made in black and white in 1953 with very cranky special effects) seem positively tame today, when computer animation can generate far more realistic monsters. But they paved the way for long-running series such as *Dr Who*, which started way back in the days of black and white TV. The earliest game shows included gems such as *Take Your Pick*, when the avuncular

Michael Miles encouraged audiences to help contestants to decide (at the tops of their voices) whether to 'open the box!' or 'take the money', and *Double Your Money*, with Hughie Green, of whom my mother was always rather distrustful. 'A bit too smarmy', was her verdict.

I was always particularly keen on the wildlife programmes. The very first ones had to be broadcast from TV studios, with experts introducing us to creatures that were considered docile enough to be handled, live, in front of hot lights. We always lived in hopes that they'd bite, escape or do a poo, and a satisfactory number did. George Cansdale was the TV animal expert in the 1950s and 1960s—he looked rather like a bank-manager in his grey suit—but the man most people remember is Johnny Morris, who played the part of a zookeeper at Bristol Zoo. He was famous for putting words into animals' mouths and imitating their 'voices'. Anthropomorphizing is frowned on today—'it removes the animals' dignity'—but we found it very amusing to hear what the camel, elephant or some small furry rodent might be thinking, and to hear its thoughts being spoken out loud in a funny voice. And it made a lot of us kids interested in animals we might never otherwise have heard of.

But as wildlife filming advanced, viewers found it far more riveting to 'travel' with the cameras to parts of the world and see creatures that few of us had ever even seen in a zoo. We were entranced by Peter Scott and his series *Look*; we joined intrepid Armand and Michaela Denis *On Safari* and visited the strange undersea world of Hans and Lotte Hass or Jacques Cousteau—breathtaking stuff. David Attenborough's *Zoo Quest* series introduced us to

219

fantastic things like Komodo dragons and birds of paradise, with glimpses of dangerous-looking native tribesmen dressed in feathers and paint and not much else. I simply couldn't get enough of it.

But my most regular not-to-be missed viewing was on Friday nights, when everything stopped, as far as I was concerned, for Percy Thrower's *Gardening Club*. No sooner had he hung his tweed jacket up on the back of the greenhouse door, I'd be agog to see what this week would bring. Would he be taking geranium cuttings? Potting up chrysanths or planting dahlias? It was a real education. I was grateful for everything I learnt in Percy's capable hands in later years, even when I discovered that his on-screen greenhouse didn't have any glass in it—the studio cameras and crew would have been reflected in it, which would have ruined the shots.

Films and cinema

Going to the pictures—better known as 'the flicks'—was a favourite Saturday afternoon pastime for teenagers and children old enough to be allowed in on their own. You met your friends outside and then all sat together, with some sweets if you could afford them. Midweek matinees were the place mothers took young children as a treat, but evening performances were the territory of adults, with courting couples occupying the double seats on the back row. Well, they didn't go to watch the film anyway.

Our local cinemas were the smart, shiny, white, art-deco fronted Essoldo and more downmarket Grove Cinema situated in a backstreet. Many towns had several—Odeon and Granada had branches everywhere. There were still a few scruffy small backstreet cinemas, like ours, known as fleapits for very good reason, though they started closing down rapidly once the public became accustomed to the glossy interiors of the big cinema chains. A trip to the cinema was one of the few regular outings for many families. The fifties was the last of the grand old days of the Hollywood movies; they were still making major musicals, romances and thrillers, with glamorous stars such as Cary Grant, Elizabeth Taylor, Richard Burton, David Niven and Bette Davis, and epics, such as *Cleopatra*, *Ben Hur* and *The Ten Commandments*, were must-sees. But we had a huge British film industry at the time, centred just west of London, turning out the Ealing Comedies (*The Lavender Hill Mob*, *The Titfield Thunderbolt* and *The Ladykillers* to name but three), Hammer Horror Films (*Frankenstein*, *Dracula* and *The Mummy*) and a long string of *Carry On* films which made stars of Sid James, Hattie Jacques, Kenneth Williams and Barbara Windsor—the first one was *Carry On Sergeant*, made in 1958 and very risqué since it showed a man's naked bottom, albeit very briefly. Mind you, my mother steered me clear of the Grove Cinema when it advertised something called *Naked as Nature Intended*. I never knew why . . .

Cinemas changed their films every week to encourage regulars to keep coming back. Ticket prices ranged from 9d to 2/6d depending on where you sat. The best seats were up in the balcony; downstairs, however, was where most people went, and the cheapest seats of all were in the rows right at the very front, where you had to crane your neck to look up at the screen. But you had very good value for money. A full performance ran for several hours since you started off with a newsreel and a B movie, before the main feature film started. In the interval you'd watch a few adverts, thoughtfully provided by Pearl and Dean, and buy a 'drink on a stick' (nothing more than a frozen orange lolly at a fancy price) from the usherette who came down the aisles carrying a laden tray of sweets, ice creams and packets of salted nuts to sustain hungry film-goers. There were cigarettes, too. Many films were watched through a veil of smoke. The performance ended with a roll of drums to give you time to stow your litter and stand up for the national anthem.

Popular music

As a small child, light music was hugely popular with all age groups, on the radio, on TV variety shows and as records. Whole families listened together to crooners such as Bing Crosby, Perry Como, Michael Holliday and later Val Doonican, and the sort of songs you'd heard in the movies, performed by stars such as Doris Day. They also liked Mantovani ('Charmaine') or records made by TV favourites such as Russ Conway. His 'China Tea' was the very first record I ever bought with my own money. Bless!

It wasn't until teenagers started to find their own voice, so to speak, that they invented their own forms of music, and what stood out was its strong rhythmic beat and lyrics that most adults found rather worrying when they could understand them at all. 'That racket' was how most people's parents

Adam Faith.

usually dismissed the sort of music teenagers liked. Which was fine by us, since we were just learning what it was like to be ourselves.

Skiffle was a home-made sort of rock 'n' roll performed by a group of lads with primitive instruments. One played a guitar—the acoustic sort, not the sort that needed plugging in to a barrage of amplifiers and speakers; another played an old-fashioned washboard with thimbles on his fingers—the sort of thing that was just being slung out from most kitchens when they were being modernized—and a third twanged a home-made bass, made from a wooden tea chest with a broom handle fixed to it bearing a single string. The idea was to copy skiffle's idols Lonnie Donegan and Joe Brown as closely as possible. The words of their songs were often distinctly strange: 'Does your chewing gum lose its flavour on the bed post overnight?' and 'My old man's a dustman'. Bernard Cribbins had a song about a hole in the ground: 'they

223

Cliff Richard.

were digging it round when it oughta be square'. Adults were baffled, but I think that was the whole idea.

Elvis Presley was controversial—after all, he was American, awfully loud, a bit flashy and considered rather daring, if not positively suggestive, because of his 'indecent' hip gyrations. But we had our own home-grown stalwarts who didn't offend the aunties quite so much: Cliff Richard (who started as plain Harry Webb singing in Hertfordshire pubs and was still having hit songs more than 50 years later) and Tommy Steele (originally Tommy Hicks, best known for 'Little White Bull' and 'Rock with the Caveman'). And we had Adam Faith and his hit 'What Do You Want if You Don't Want Money?'—interestingly, he later moved into a career in finance. Then we discovered pop. The swinging sixties brought us The Beatles, and for a while anything Liverpudlian was big. 'She Loves You' swept to the top of the hit parade and stayed there for weeks. Meanwhile teenagers were all tuning in to the pop music shows on TV to keep in touch with what we should be listening to—*The Six-Five Special* and *Ready Steady Go!* let us hear all the latest new releases, which we could then go out and buy. You didn't need to be much of a music critic—you knew that if parents disapproved, it had to be good.

Fun and games

Children had very few toys or games, so we made most of our own entertainment using little more than a vivid imagination. Most families kept a dressing-up box filled with old clothes or curtains that could be used for props for games of make-believe or impromptu theatrical performances. Nobody turned a hair at the sight of small boys trailing round the back garden wearing one of their mother's old dance dresses or draped in an off-the-shoulder chintz curtain tucked into the shorts as a pirate outfit. On fine sunny summer days we might make camps in the garden by draping old sheets or curtains over the branches of apple trees, the washing line or a wooden clothes horse. If all else failed you could use a large cardboard box— the enormous ones that appliances such as washing machines were delivered in made ideal forts. Or we'd go off out into the countryside, exploring footpaths, climbing trees, damming streams or picking wildflowers. (Yes, I know it wouldn't be allowed now, but then who'd let small kids wander off on their own today either?)

Wildlife also came in for attention. We'd go fishing in the River Wharfe, in shorts, using a net or a home-made fishing rod—I'd cut a long willow-wand, tie on cotton from one of the reels in Mum's sewing kit and fasten a bent pin to the end as a hook. I never caught anything with it, but I was a dab hand at catching minnows and bullheads with a net, and there was always the chance of a crayfish. I'd decant my catch into a jam jar so I could take a good look before letting it go. Or I'd take our dog Cindy off to the woods for a spot of birdwatching, identifying things I saw with the help of Ladybird books and ticking off each new 'find' on a master-list. Some of the slightly unrulier kids might do a spot of scrumping in the apple season or take birds' eggs in spring, both of which involved a little gentle trespassing. This could earn you a thick ear or a visit to your father from an enraged farmer or the local bobby—not to be recommended. Too much of this and you'd give the whole family a bad name.

Among the more organized activities we had Brownies, Wolf Cubs, Girl Guides and Boy Scouts which most children joined at the time. We all enjoyed collecting the various badges which showed our proficiency at tasks like tracking and knots, but the great bonus was you could go away to camp in the summer and spend a week under canvas. This was great fun (when you got over the homesickness) and quite a change from everyday life—we'd spend our evenings singing round the campfire, heating twists of dough, and cooking bangers and beans in billycans that we'd eat off tin plates without adults reminding us to wash our hands all the time.

The Church also had its own activities. There

was the youth group and the choir, which gave me my first taste of performing in public. But don't imagine choirboys to be angelic, despite their looks; most of us went into the choir stalls on Sundays with a catapult in our pocket and a supply of comics and bubblegum to while away the long, boring sermons.

Children didn't need a lot of 'stuff' to be happy. We might have a few comics such as *The Beano*, *The Dandy*, *Swift*, *Eagle*, *The Hotspur* or *Wizard*, and magazines like the *War Picture Library* or *Look and Learn*. If our dad took a newspaper we'd turn to Andy Capp and the Giles cartoons. Dad got the *Giles Annual* every year. I got *Rupert*. You'd have a few hobbies—a lot of lads made model aircraft from Airfix kits, though real enthusiasts started from scratch with balsa wood, a tube of strange-smelling balsa cement and a Stanley knife. Girls would dress doll shapes in cut-out clothes that had tabs that you bent over the shoulders to make them stay on.

If you were lucky, you might be given a camera; I had a Brownie 127. It was all black and white film in those days; you only got eight pictures on a reel, and since it was rather an expensive hobby you tended to use your few shots very carefully. You waited with baited breath to get them back from the chemist to see how they came out and would be very disappointed if family shots ended up with the heads cut off. Being keen on wildlife, I had a few books on the subject: *The Observer Book of Wild Animals*, *The Observer Book of Pond Life*, three bird books in the Ladybird series, and a copy of *British Bird Life*, by W. Percival Westell, written in 1905 and given to me by our old next-door neighbour

Mrs Cunnington who realized I was interested in anything that crawled, fluttered, swam or grew.

Every spring I trawled the icy waters of the tarn on Ilkley Moor for frogspawn, which reminded me of the sago pudding we almost had to be force-fed at school dinners, and then watched the black full stops turn into commas and the tadpoles into baby frogs. I was also keen on wildflowers, and besides looking for them when I was out exploring the countryside, I'd pick some specimens to press, which was the best way to preserve them. The idea was to open the flower out and 'trap it' in place between several sheets of newspaper, then put it underneath the rug that ran between the sitting room and the kitchen. After a few days the flowers were totally flat and dry and I'd stick them into a big book rather like a stamp album, with sheets of tissue paper from our daily loaf laid between them. I won a school prize for my collection, which ran to *two* entire albums. I still have them, complete with my first attempts at joined-up writing with a spidery hand in fountain-pen ink.

Collecting things was a popular pastime, especially as it could be done on the cheap. We'd collect almost anything: old bus tickets, the front of cigarette packets or jam-jar labels. Stamp collecting was something a lot of boys went in for. You'd often start by collecting unusual foreign stamps that arrived on envelopes posted to friends or relatives, but in time you'd graduate to buying stamps from adverts in the backs of magazines—you could get lots for very little money. You'd stick them into an album in neat rows with see-through stamp hinges. I did it for a while, but lost heart after not too long, and so most of my stamps ended up in a tin waiting to be stuck in. It's fair to say that most collections were rather short lived—collecting ran in phases, and those 'in the know' were always moving on to something new by the time the also-rans had cottoned on.

Handicrafts were always popular. A lot of kids would be given *The Hobbies Annual* for Christmas and it kept them going all year, but all sorts of tips for home-made crafts came out of magazines. It was amazing what you could do if you put your mind to it. I used to make miniature gardens by putting an old 78rpm record in hot water, and when it was soft enough to bend without breaking, I pulled the sides up to make a bowl complete with drainage hole in the bottom. With a few plants and some bits of shell or stone, these made nice presents to give to aunties and other deserving adults. Some kids did the same by melting plastic LPs over clay flower pots in the oven. That worked quite well, too, but if you left them for too long it did make the kitchen smell a bit funny, and your mother would be cross about the congealed mess next time she wanted to do some baking. And if you'd purloined a record she still treasured, you were in hot water for weeks.

If nothing better came along, you'd fill your time by going out to play and perhaps making a fire out of old bits of rubbish in someone's backyard or inventing your own games with lead soldiers, toy farm animals or Dinky cars in a heap of sand, which could be landscaped to represent anything from a desert to a battlefield or a bit of the Wild West. For a while there was a great craze for lads to make go-karts. What you needed was an orange box, which you got from the greengrocer, and a set of pram wheels, scrounged from the back of someone's garage. Put the two together with some strings for elementary steerage, and you could sit or lie on top and race downhill in the middle of the road or go crashing along the paths scattering everything in your wake. Naturally some kids came terrible croppers and after a few loose teeth, grazed legs and shattered undercarriages, parents tended to step in and ban go-karts—at least, until next time.

But quite a lot of children got together just to 'muck about' outside in the street. It was perfectly safe since there wasn't much traffic. You only needed two or three friends to play hide-and-seek or kick-can (an improved form of hide-and-seek in which, when you were found, you had to run from your hiding place and kick the can before the person who found you had the chance to kick it himself). You could play cricket using a wicket chalked onto a wall (we used the local bus garage, which was at the end of our road) or football, with only one goal, made by piling up everyone's jerseys in two heaps. Making an absorbing day's fun out of absolutely nothing might have sounded very dull—deprived, even—by today's standards, but it was just the same for everyone we mixed with. We learnt to fall back on our own resources instead of expecting our parents to keep buying expensive toys we'd soon become bored with or break—or so we were told.

Smoking? Ah, yes. Just the one. A Woodbine round the back of the bus garage, followed by a packet of Polo mints to take the smell away before going home. Some tried more, but only on the quiet, and never in front of their parents. I just got

230

queasy.

And, of course, there were parties. We'd have them for just about any special occasion. One we always celebrated was Bonfire Night. We made a guy out of Dad's oldest and worst set of work overalls, despite his protests, then all the neighbours would come round, and we'd bake potatoes in the embers of our bonfire and eat them along with parkin (treacly cake) and mugs of cocoa while we set off our fireworks. It was mostly just a few rockets, which we stood in milk bottles to be lit, plus the odd Roman candle stuck in the garden or Catherine wheels nailed to the fence. Small kids would be given lighted sparklers to hold, though they'd be told to wear gloves to protect their hands. You couldn't get the big high-explosive jobs you see people letting off today. At least, not on our budget. We mostly bought modest-sized mixed boxes from the newsagents, and in those days we let them off only on 5 November or, if it rained, the following Friday or Saturday night was allowed. It was an unwritten rule. The night before Bonfire Night was Mischief Night, when we'd ring doorbells and run away or throw dustbin lids down into backyards. We were only caught once. My ear did sting.

Birthdays were always a good excuse for a party. You'd have tea with cake and jelly and blancmange, followed by party games—the traditional sort, such as pass the parcel, musical chairs and pin the tail on the donkey, with a few songs round the piano. Sardines or spin the bottle were a tad more risqué, involving close encounters with the opposite sex, and the opportunity for a spot of snogging. But by then we were in our teens. If it all sounds a

POCKET MONEY

I was given a shilling a week by my parents in the late 1950s, which was about average compared to most of my friends (a child of a well-to-do family might get as much as three bob), but what with hobbies, seeds and things to buy for my bit of garden it didn't go far at all.

Most children liked to earn a bit of extra spending money. If you didn't mind getting up early you could put in a few hours' work before school, either helping the milkman or doing a paper round. Vacancies were highly sought-after, so you had to be jolly reliable or someone else would soon get your job. I opted for a paper round: for a couple of years or so I delivered 30 papers over a hilly two-mile course, five days a week for a shilling a day. It was hard going since the big canvas bag was pretty heavy when it held a full load, and I was only four-foot six at the time, but on pay day I felt like a millionaire. Singing in the choir was a good little earner for me, too, even though it meant turning out in a purple cassock and long white surplice with a big frilly ruff. I did it for eight years. All the choirboys got sixpence a week, paid in a lump sum every six months, and for singing at weddings we were each given half a crown. Bell-ringers were paid five bob for weddings. Riches!

It's not that we were money-grabbing, but times were hard and if you wanted anything 'extra' you had to find a way to fund it

> yourself. We knew it was no good pestering parents or relatives for hand-outs that we wouldn't get. Times were too hard for such extravagances. But it didn't do us any harm—it taught us to stand on our own two feet. It also taught us the value of money; before throwing 6d around on sweets, you thought of the effort you'd taken to earn it and decided if the outlay was really worthwhile.

bit basic, a bit innocent, well it was, but we had a wonderful time.

Adult fun and games

Kids weren't the only ones who liked to go out and have fun. Adults had their own forms of amusement, outside the home.

Bingo, or housey-housey as it was first called, was the big new thing; housewives sometimes blew the whole week's housekeeping money at the local bingo hall. The caller would shout 'eyes down, look in' to start the session, then he'd call out the numbers he drew with an amusing addition: 'legs 11', 'two fat ladies, 88', and so forth, until you were first to make a complete row or a full house. It was a total mystery to us kids but clearly very addictive.

More refined ladies went out to whist drives where you could win anything from a box of toffees to a live hen, hanging upside down from its feet which were tied with string (incredibly it took years before someone decided this might be a bit unkind and stopped the practice).

Village fêtes often held a beetle drive. Players

each took turns to throw a dice; you needed a six to start, then you had to assemble a whole beetle from individual body parts that you 'won' according to the numbers turned up with each succeeding throw of the dice—first the torso, then the head, then the legs and the 'feelers'. The first person to assemble their complete beetle, in the right order, won. The prizes were nothing much; you did it for the fun of taking part.

WHAT WAS MAKING THE NEWS?

Disasters/scandals

1958   Thalidomide disaster. A 'harmless' pill for morning sickness given to expectant mothers results in hundreds of deformed babies.

1963   Great Train Robbery nets more than £2 million. The villains escape with the loot.

1963   President Kennedy shot dead during a motorcade through Dallas, Texas. Almost everyone from the time remembers where they were when they heard the news.

1963   The Profumo Affair. The Secretary of State for War, John Profumo, discovers he has been sharing a mistress, Christine Keeler, with a Russian spy and resigns amidst concerns over national security. The press have a field day over goings-on at Cliveden that trickle out as Keeler and her friend Mandy Rice-Davis give evidence in court.

1963–65 The Moors murders, which took place uncomfortably close to home, with bodies thought to have been buried on Saddleworth Moor. Ian Brady and Myra Hindley are still thought of as some of our most notorious murderers today.

1966 The Aberfan disaster. A slag heap slips down a Welsh hillside near Merthyr Tydfil and obliterates a primary school full of children.

The Cold War

Poor relations with the Soviet Union continue throughout the 1950s and early 1960s and lead to nuclear proliferation. CND (the Campaign for Nuclear Disarmament) want to 'ban the bomb', bearing the familiar logo on their banners at protests and demonstrations. Soviet spies are recruited at top universities, and spy scandals regularly fill the news.

1960 Gary Powers is shot down over Russia in his U-2 spy plane.

1961 The Berlin wall is built.

1962 The Cuban Missile Crisis, during which the world came within a whisker of nuclear war; nuclear bunkers and fall-out shelters appear, largely for government officials.

The Space Race

1957 Russians put the first-ever satellite, Sputnik 1, in space, and a Russian dog, Laika, follows a month later.

1959 A Soviet rocket hits the moon; Russians photograph the dark side of the moon.

1961 Russians make the first manned space flight, with Yuri Gagarin doing an orbit of Earth; not to be outdone the Americans send Alan Shepard up and back three weeks later but without doing a circuit.

1962 John Glenn orbits the Earth.

1963 Russia puts the first woman in space.

1966 The unmanned Gemini 9 lands on the moon.

1969 The first man walks on the moon; Neil Armstrong says 'one small step for man, one giant leap for mankind'.

1971 Astronauts drive on the moon.

Great British achievements

1954 Roger Bannister breaks the four-minute mile.

1955 Donald Campbell breaks the world water-speed record with *Bluebird* on Ullswater at an average speed of 202.32mph.

1958 The hovercraft is invented by a Brit, Christopher Cockerell.

1960 Francis Chichester crosses the Atlantic solo in record time in his 39-foot sloop

Gypsy Moth III; in true British style he took a dinner jacket with him but it went mouldy.

1966   England win the World Cup beating Germany at Wembley Stadium, under captain Bobby Moore.

1967   Francis Chichester, aged 65, completes a solo round-the-world voyage in Gypsy Moth IV after 119 days at sea, including a non-stop passage from Sydney to Plymouth, despite having lung cancer. He was knighted.

1967   The first supersonic aircraft, Concorde, capable of travelling at speeds of 2,000mph, rolls out of Toulouse airport. It is a joint Anglo-French venture.

1968   'I'm Backing Britain' campaign starts.

1968   Alec Rose, a 59-year-old greengrocer, returns to Portsmouth in his small ketch *Lively Lady* after sailing round the world—28,500 miles—in 354 days.

1969   Tony Jacklin becomes the first British golfer to win a major US golf championship for 18 years; Britain's Ann Jones beats American Billie Jean King to win Wimbledon.

1969   The first North Sea oil starts to flow.

Theatre and the arts

1952   Agatha Christie's play *The Mousetrap* opens at the Ambassadors Theatre on the evening of 25 November.

1958   John Betjeman's *Collected Poems* about

old railways, suburban gentility and the tennis-playing Miss Joan Hunter Dunn poke fun at class-ridden British society.

1960   The Lady Chatterley trial declares D H Lawrence's notorious book *Lady Chatterley's Lover* is not obscene, despite the prosecuting council asking the jury: 'Is this a book you would wish your wife or your servant to read?' The day after the trial Penguin Books sell 200,000 copies priced 3s 6d as people rush to find out what the fuss is all about.

1964   Shakespeare's quatercentenary (400th anniversary); Maggie Smith and Lawrence Olivier star in *Othello* at the National Theatre.

Obits

1961   Sir Thomas Beecham, conductor, dies aged 81; he inherited a fortune from Beecham's Pills and spent it funding orchestras including the Royal Philharmonic.

1964   Ian Fleming, author of the James Bond books, dies. Several have already become huge box-office successes as films.

1965   Sir Winston Churchill dies and, after a state funeral at St Paul's, is buried in the churchyard near the family home of Blenheim.

1967   Donald Campbell dies during his

attempt on the world water-speed record on Coniston Water when *Bluebird* somersaults at 300mph. His body is not found, only his mascot, a teddy bear.

1972   The Duke of Windsor, who gave up the throne to marry Wallace Simpson, dies.

1973   Nancy Mitford dies; author of *The Pursuit of Love* and co-originator of U and non-U, showing how people give away their social background by careless use of words, for example it's U (upper class) to say pudding, and non-U (lower class) to say sweet.

1975   Sir P. G. Wodehouse dies, author of stories about Blandings Castle and the gentleman's gentleman, Jeeves, and his master Bertie Wooster.

1976   Agatha Christie, author of 80 detective books including the Miss Marple and Poirot series, dies aged 85. The lights are dimmed outside St Martin's Theatre where *The Mousetrap* is in its 25th year. Sales of her books topped a record £300 million, making her Britain's richest author.

1976   Percy Shaw, the inventor of catseyes, dies. In the tradition of all the best British inventors, he had thought the idea up while coming home from the pub.

1984   Sir John Betjeman, poet, social commentator and architectural enthusiast, dies; he championed 'everything threatened by ghastly good taste'. It was he who said: 'Come friendly bombs and fall on Slough, it isn't fit for humans now.'

1984　J. B. Priestley dies; his favourite subject was 'The English'. He was a great arbiter of Yorkshire common sense.

1984　Richard Burton, coal miner's son and actor from Wales, dies. He'd been married five times including twice to Elizabeth Taylor whom he met on the set of *Cleopatra*.

1985　Roy Plomley, host of Desert Island Discs, dies; the programme has run regularly on BBC radio since 1941.

CHAPTER 9

THE WAY WE WERE AT HOME

While men went out to work, daily life for most women revolved around the home. This was the heyday of the housewife; my mother might not have thought of herself as a domestic goddess, but that's what she'd be seen as today. Domestic matters such as cooking, shopping, cleaning and children filled her day, and the days of women like her all around the country. Housewives were extremely thrifty; they had to be because money was always tight and, in any case, there were very few goods to buy in the shops. 'Make do and mend' was the order of the day, just as it had been during the War. Nothing was ever thrown away if it could be somehow re-used. Recycling was invented in the 1950s.

But in 1957 Supermac (Prime Minister Harold Macmillan) told us 'we'd never had it so good', and at last the purse strings loosened slightly, life began to ease up and a few little luxuries, new fashions and labour-saving devices began to appear. Even so the standard of living was rather slow to rise, especially for people who lived a long way from London, and things didn't really gain momentum until the swinging sixties when people began splashing out on fashionable clothing, records, cars and new furniture. At home, we didn't feel hard done by in any way; that's just how life was. We counted our blessings. Unlike a lot of people we had a car (well, a plumber's van), an indoor bathroom and central heating (both put in by Dad), and a phone (which he needed for his job). And the one thing we were never short of in our house was family feeling. It left you with a deep-rooted sense of security that no amount of fancy consumer goods could replace.

Routine chores

Running a house and family was a full-time job. The average 1950s housewife worked a 15-hour day. Most had their week well planned out; Mum's schedule ran like clockwork. Monday she did the washing; Tuesday the ironing; Wednesday and Thursday were earmarked for cleaning and Friday was baking day. Saturday would be shopping day, and on Sunday we'd all go out for a walk or a 'run' up the Dales in the van. And that was a pretty typical week for most housewives.

Each day started off much the same. One of the first jobs for Mrs 1950 would be to prepare a proper cooked breakfast for the family, and make her husband's packed lunch, which he took to work with him in a khaki bag slung over his shoulder. It would be nothing fancy. My dad usually had a flask of tea, cheese or ham sandwiches, a hard-boiled egg wrapped in waxed paper, and a Penguin biscuit, which he'd eat in his van. Then most mums would walk small children to school or send older children off on their bikes or to the bus, making sure they'd got their satchels. In cold weather, kids were sent off in thick coats, scarves and balaclava helmets, with mittens on tapes running down inside the sleeves of their coats, so they couldn't be mislaid. (If you lost them, you'd not only be cold, you'd also get told off when you got home.) With the kids out of the way, and after maybe an hour or so shopping for fresh bread, meat and vegetables, a housewife could get stuck into the day's Big Job.

Washday was particularly tough. When I was *very* small Mum still used a dolly tub, which you filled with hot soapy water, added dirty clothes, and then bashed them about with a wooden 'dolly peg' (a thing like a short-legged stool mounted on a bit of broom handle). She had to rub stains or dirty collars and cuffs on a washboard, then wring the wet clothes out by feeding them through a hand-operated mangle. Anything too delicate to stand up to this treatment had to be washed by hand using flakes of Lux soap. In Grandma's day they'd had to grate bars of soap to make their own flakes, but by now you could buy them in packets though they were too expensive to be chucked about freely. But all this came to a halt when Dad bought a washer. The early washing machines were little more than a metal tub that heated its own water, with an agitator on the side or up the centre that mixed the clothes in the suds and spared you most of the heavy manual work. It had its own motorised mangle so you just had to feed clothes through instead of cranking a handle as well, but it was very likely to grab your fingers along with the wet washing. Though it was certainly an improvement on the dolly tub, it wasn't *all that* labour saving. For a start it wasn't plumbed in; you had to shift the device out from its usual parking space under the kitchen counter, manoeuvre it alongside the sink and fill it with a bit of hose that pushed on over the kitchen taps. When the clothes had 'stewed' for long enough, you'd lift them out with long wooden tongs. After a squeeze through the wringer you rinsed them out by hand, in clean water in the sink.

It still took ages, because each load of washing had to go through the same long drawn-out process, and a house with two children could generate four or five loads at least. Most of the women along our road did their laundry on the same day so by the time I came home from school the gardens would be alive with billowing sheets, shirts, pillowcases, pinnies and bloomers—voluminous and salmon-pink in the case of all the old ladies in the street. When the whole lot was finished you had to empty the washing machine using another bit of hose that connected up to a pump in the base and squirted the water back into the sink or a bucket that had to be emptied down the drain.

However careful you were, the whole job left your kitchen full of steam and the floor awash with water, so smart housewives left 'doing the kitchen floor' until the laundry was finished, so they only had to mop the lino down once. When it was all done, they'd have a few hours' rest before there'd be dryish laundry to bring in and air ready for the next day when they set to and ironed it all. There weren't any drip-dry shirts or easy-iron clothes, and mothers took a pride in sending their family off in pristine whites and sparkling coloureds, all immaculately pressed, so they'd spend ages doing the job beautifully. Make no mistake, laundry was still hard work.

Cleaning took another two full days; jobs that only take minutes today took ages to do when you didn't have any labour-saving electrical devices. There was also far more cleaning to do in a 1950s home because coal fires created a lot of dust, and living rooms were always filled with masses of ornaments and knick-knacks, all of which had to be lovingly moved, cleaned round and then washed or dusted themselves. Wooden furniture was wax-polished every week which meant smearing on a thick lavender-scented goo, buffing it up and rubbing hard till it shone—there were none of the modern products you simply spray on and dust off. Hearth rugs were taken outside to be shaken out down the garden, and wooden floors and kitchen lino were swept and polished till they sparkled.

In between all of this there would sometimes be tradesmen to deal with. The insurance man called every week for a small payment, which was the only way most working people saved. We were with Pearl Assurance, but Prudential did much the same thing. The coalman called every two or three weeks. Coal was delivered in sacks and was shot down a chute into your cellar or tipped into a concrete coal bunker in the back garden. A selection of tradesmen did door-to-door rounds selling wet fish, meat or greengroceries, so you had to be home when they called, and the lady of the house was expected to keep proper household accounts so her husband could see where her housekeeping money went.

Mum used to set small sums aside in tiny cash boxes from Woolworths for each individual tradesman each week, so it was ready when they called for their money. All this had to be done before getting her children's tea and cooking an evening meal for her husband when he came home. Then she'd put the children to bed and read them a story. Ours were often Beatrix Potter, which I still look back on with great affection. I've often wondered if those bedtime brushes with Peter Rabbit, the gardener and the lettuces didn't plant a subliminal seed that grew into a horticultural career.

If a fifties housewife found herself with any spare time, she'd use it profitably to catch up with mending, darning, sewing, knitting or dressmaking. It was the only way to make a small income stretch a long way. You didn't throw away old or damaged clothes: they'd be mended or altered; you patched worn-out trousers when the knees went through and darned wool socks when they had holes. Shirt collars were detachable, so you could launder them separately if the rest of the shirt was still clean enough to wear again or replace them when they looked threadbare, instead of throwing the entire garment away. A lot of ingenuity went into turning hems up or down to make the same skirt or pair of trousers last growing children several years; even so children's clothes were passed down in the family until they couldn't be used any more. School uniforms had to have Cash's name tapes sewn in the backs, so they wouldn't be lost—schools insisted on it—so just before the start of a new school year there'd be a flurry of unpicking and resewing when all the regulation blazers, skirts and trousers changed hands. We couldn't afford Cash's, so Mum made her own from small pieces of white tape on which were written 'TITCHMARSH' in indelible ink. They were sewn into all of our school clothes. How we yearned for 'proper' labels.

Young kids always complained that they never had anything new, only other people's hand-me-downs. But that's just how it was. A housewife made the most of her own clothes and those of her children—girls did better out of the deal since it was easier to make skirts and summer dresses than shorts or trousers. But Mum was very good at it;

she even made dance dresses and winter coats. A keen dressmaker would usually start with a dress-length of fabric that she'd bought cheaply as an offcut, and then she'd buy a pattern or, better still, borrow one from a friend. Mum did a lot of this. I can still see Patons' tissue patterns spread out over the rug in the front room pinned to fabric; these were rearranged to make the best use of the material before she took the plunge and cut it out, then the bits were sewn together on an old Singer sewing machine with a handle that was turned by hand. Later she acquired from the saleroom at the bottom of the street an advanced, but clanking, model which featured a foot treadle and this turned a flywheel via a big, strong rubber band. Difficult bits or fancy stitching were done by hand. Any leftover bits of fabric were saved up in a ragbag and used as cleaning cloths, while the tougher bits were made into rag rugs or used to stuff rolls of fabric to stop draughts coming in under the doors in winter. Very little was ever thrown away—we were a generation of born and bred recyclers.

Mum's meals

Meals were the heart of family life. People had three square meals a day, eaten round the table. We'd never have dreamt of 'grazing' throughout the day as people do now—regular mealtimes brought the family together. By sitting down together for knife-and-fork meals, children learned the art of conversation and good table manners, adults discussed plans for weekends and evenings, family outings or visits, and everyone could chip in, besides exchanging news about what they'd been doing all day. It was all very sociable. In any case nobody snacked or ate between meals. It wasn't just for the sake of good digestion, as elderly aunts would have had us believe. Food was still in short supply for several years after the War was over (meat was still on ration when I was very small), so you made it go round as far as possible by making filling, thrifty meals—expensive main ingredients were well padded out with plenty of potatoes and pastry. Nobody would ever have thought of helping themselves to a tasty snack out of the fridge any time they felt peckish; even a slice of cheese or a cold sausage would have been a vital ingredient that mother was relying on to make the next meal. You didn't so much as pinch a biscuit out of the biscuit barrel on the sideboard; you'd wait to be offered one from a plate with a cup of tea mid-morning or mid-afternoon, sitting down in the kitchen or living room.

As for eating outside in the street—it just wasn't done. It wasn't good manners to let other people see you munching and stuffing your face. Even when it was only sweets, you usually had to wait until you got home to eat them. The only possible exception was the occasional ice cream on the beach or while you were walking along the prom, when you were on holiday at the seaside. When the ice-cream van came down the street on a summer Sunday, you'd still carry the cornet home before you ate it—though you were allowed to lick off any drips that threatened to deface your Sunday best clothes.

The week's meals didn't vary all that much. You'd always have a fairly good idea what you'd be getting to eat on any given day. Sunday dinner

*Puddings were wholesome and filling,
even if they were sometimes made from
the most basic ingredients.*

at 1pm was a big family occasion and every now and then we'd have company—a nearby aunt or a granny would come round, and the children would be dressed in their Sunday best. This was the most elaborate meal of the week—the Sunday roast. Chicken was expensive and a special treat; there was no factory farming, so the only chickens available were reared the old-fashioned way, slowly and naturally. We only had one at Easter or on special occasions.

Most Sundays it would be roast lamb, pork or beef, and we'd have a modest-sized joint that would feed four with some left over for the following week. Mum would make proper gravy with the meat juices in the bottom of the roasting pan—nothing out of a packet—and the first course would be two small Yorkshire puddings with gravy. The main course would be a slice or two of meat (Dad

249

carved and Mum always had the outside bit, which she liked best) with roast potatoes and one or two veg, bolstered up with another individual Yorkshire pudding. The story was that the person who ate the most Yorkshire pudding for starters could have the most meat with the main course—the trick being that the person who had had the most Yorkshire pudding wanted less meat. Neat, eh? This would be followed by pudding, which was nearly always apple or plum pie—all using as much produce from the garden as possible, and in winter it would be made using bottled fruit from the larder.

On Monday, the leftovers from the Sunday joint were minced up to make shepherd's pie or rissoles. These were a delicious mixture of minced-up meat and potatoes fried in the pan. A thrifty housewife bought mince but she'd have worried about what a butcher might have put into it; he'd certainly have economized and not used the very best cuts.

Tuesdays', Wednesdays' and Thursdays' main meals might be sausages, toad in the hole, macaroni cheese, tripe and onions or something of the sort, but we always had fish on Fridays. Fried with chips or steamed with mash, it was traditional—and in those days it was still compulsory for Catholics. For pudding there would be stewed fruit and custard (living in Yorkshire we had lots of rhubarb). It was only on special occasions like children's parties that we might have a real treat—jelly or blancmange (milky jelly) and ice cream. The fashionable dessert, for adults only, was sherry trifle. It was made from layers of stale sponge cake soaked in a little sweet sherry and tinned fruit left to set firmly in jelly, topped with custard and decorated on top with cream (on special occasions) or just a sprinkling of violently coloured 'hundreds and thousands'. It was glamorous yet thrifty, a good way to use up bits and pieces in the bottom of your cake-tin that might otherwise have been thrown away. Sherry trifle remained the height of sophistication until knocked off its perch by Black Forest gateau in the 1960s.

There were very few convenience foods on sale in shops, mostly just a few cans of fruit or tinned processed peas. You could find the odd packet of cake mix, but they were frowned on by most housewives, who found the idea faintly insulting; the general feeling was that only a bad mother would take short cuts of that sort, however busy she might be. No, she'd bake once or twice a week and turn out all her own jam tarts, fairy cakes and scones for the children's teas, plus Victoria sponges and fruit pies for puddings. (Well, it was a waste of expensive gas or electricity to heat the oven up just for one cake or pie, so a thrifty housewife always batched the job up and made sure the oven was *full* if she was going to use it at all.)

And if she was a bit short of ingredients for a midweek pudding, thrifty mothers made 'plate pies'—an old wartime recipe that nobody under a certain age has ever eaten today. A layer of pastry was laid over a greased round tin plate, then it was smeared all over with a lick of jam, and another layer of pastry was put over the top to make something like a giant, round jam sandwich. When it had been cooked it was sliced into wedges and eaten hot with lots of custard. Very filling and very cheap. The only instant food commonly used was custard powder—Bird's—but it still took more making than opening a tin of today's ready-made custard, since you had to mix it with milk and then bring it slowly to the boil, stirring it constantly so it didn't turn lumpy. If it all sounds a bit dull and unimaginative it was, but it was filling, home-cooked and wholesome.

One thing 1950s mothers were very good at was using up leftovers. They reappeared in all sorts of inventive ways. Dripping would be saved in enamel bowls after cooking the Sunday joint. Bread and dripping (a thick slice of bread spread with beef dripping and seasoned with plenty of salt) was delicious as a snack, a bit unhealthy you might think, but not when you were out all day in the cold doing heavy manual work. As kids we sat elbow to elbow on the back doorstep eating it for our elevenses. Dripping was also saved for frying—eggs, chips, bacon, sausages all tasted far better cooked in beef dripping—and a pot of home-saved dripping was always on hand when you cooked roast Sunday lunches, while bottles of cooking oil hardly existed.

Cold meat would be recycled as rissoles, stuffed marrow or corned-beef hash with a fried egg on top—as delicious today as ever it was. Cold cooked veg were turned into soup; potato and cabbage were mashed up and fried to make bubble and squeak—people often cooked too much on purpose, so they had the makings of the next day's meal. Stale bread had 101 different uses; we'd have bread-and-butter pudding, or it would be used in home-made stuffing for a chicken, or crumbled and dried in the oven to make crispy crumbs for coating fried fish. Nobody felt hard up; it was just what you did. In any case, there wasn't much alternative. Anything that you *really* couldn't re-use yourself or give to the family pets went into a

252

COOKERY BOOKS AND TV COOKS

In the 1960s housewives started having access to a slightly wider range of more interesting ingredients, and tastes changed, cooking started to become more creative and housewives (particularly those living in the posher parts of London and the well-off home counties) started to look for their inspiration beyond granny's tried and tested recipes or ideas for economical suppers in women's magazines.

The well-travelled food writer Elizabeth David published her groundbreaking book *French Provincial Cooking* in 1960, which started a few adventurous souls along the road to cooking 'foreign food' at home. On TV, Fanny and Johnny Craddock were known for their rather starchy delivery and formal food ('here's one I cooked earlier'), not to mention Fanny's dismissive treatment of her distinctly hen-pecked husband, who was probably one of the last people to wear a monocle on television. They were soon joined by Galloping Gourmet Graham Kerr with his far more bright and breezy style and his habit of inviting people from the audience to taste his offerings at the end of the programme, accompanied by a 'quick slurp'—the first encounter many northern folk had with wine.

special bucket along with potato peelings and other bits and pieces, and the contents would be collected regularly by 'the swill man' and used to feed to pigs.

Nothing was wasted. A post-war housewife could have kept her family for a week on what her modern counterpart throws away. (Today it's reckoned people waste a third of the food they buy.) All I can say is that very few children had a weight problem, and we were always ready for our next meal, whatever it might be. A fussy eater wouldn't have stood a chance.

Christmas

Christmas dinner was always shared with as many of your extended family as you could muster; all the nearby aunts and grannies were expected to come round for such a big occasion. It was the one day you always knew there'd be more food than you could possibly eat, and the one day that a family row could be guaranteed. On a good year it would be brief and easily smoothed over.

The star of the feast was the turkey. There were no such things as small birds in those days; they were all enormous, and families took great pride in having the biggest one they could get. A 20lb turkey was about average, but you'd often end up with a monster weighing 30lb that would hardly fit in the oven. (We were given one by a grateful customer of Dad's that Mum had to put in standing on its end.) More usually, you'd collect it from the butcher's shop on Christmas Eve or ideally have it delivered. There was no messing about trying to defrost it since all the turkeys were sold fresh; they'd have been plucked and drawn, but they weren't exactly what you'd call oven-ready. A housewife had to spend a bit of time on it. First the head and feet had to be removed, any last few feathers were plucked by hand—strong stubs of pin feathers often had to be pulled out with pliers—and if the carcase still looked a touch fluffy any remaining down would be singed off with a lighted spill. Finally, the inside of the body cavity would be wiped out and filled with home-made sage, onion and sausage-meat stuffing, and the bird would be trussed up with string so it fitted into its own special giant roasting tin. It would be left overnight on a marble shelf in the pantry or larder. On Christmas morning mothers always came downstairs early, around 6am, to turn the oven on, since a monster bird packed solid with stuffing took a good six hours or more to cook properly.

But in any case she needed an early start, since there was so much cooking to do. The turkey giblets would be boiled up to make the gravy. There was bread sauce to make, from real breadcrumbs, milk and an onion studded with whole cloves—no instant packet of ready-mix—and mountains of veg to peel. The Christmas pudding would have been made anything up to six months in advance and left to mature in a huge pudding basin. It would be dug out of its biscuit tin at the back of the larder, wrapped in a linen pudding cloth, and boiled for several hours in the largest saucepan. Meanwhile there'd be custard and brandy butter to make. It was all go.

Christmas had its own set of rituals which were much the same for most families and haven't changed all that much even today. It all started at bedtime on Christmas Eve when we hung stockings up over the fireplace for Santa and left him a mince pie and a glass of sherry on a plate by the hearth, along with a carrot for Rudolph. Then we retired to bed in a state of immense excitement. I wonder how we ever managed to get to sleep. At dawn, there'd be a mad rush to see what was in our Christmas stocking. We'd find a few small wrapped gifts, plus the inevitable handful of walnuts and a tangerine in the toe. Then it was up and dressed in Sunday best and off to church. Back home the adults would all have a glass of sherry, which left the old aunts a bit merry.

Then came the big moment when we were finally allowed to open our *main presents* under the Christmas tree. These days most people buy anything they need during the course of the year and they'll have lots of treats all the time, but in those days you waited till Christmas for virtually everything. Even so, people didn't throw money around too much—well, times were tight. Most kids would have one big present from their parents. You might get a second-hand bike (mine always came from the saleroom where Mum bought the sitting-room furniture) or perhaps a clockwork train set—it was mostly Hornby and Tri-ang at the time. If your uncle or dad was good with his hands, a little girl might be given a home-made doll's house, and boys might get a home-made fort or a zoo which you'd stock with lead soldiers or animals. I had both at various times; Dad also made me a garage for my Dinky cars, and since I kept tadpoles each summer he also made me a vivarium to keep the current year's crop of baby frogs in, with a cut-glass sugarbowl 'borrowed' from Mum for their pond.

There'd also be a sprinkling of smaller presents

256

We were always happy with whatever we were given (honest!).

from uncles and aunts, such as Dinky toys, Corgi cars, Matchbox models or Airfix kits and books— most of the kids' comics produced annuals which were like bumper hard-backed editions, but a lot of Christmas presents tended to be things you needed like new clothes or shoes. We were usually very happy with whatever we were given. Usually. Grown-ups only had one or two presents each—and they were always something 'sensible'—but, as they always said, Christmas was really for the children. Even so we were expected to keep a list of who'd given us what and send them each a polite thank-you note straight afterwards.

Before the excitement of all your new presents wore off, along came the next big treat: dinner. (They called it lunch down south we were told, but we had breakfast, dinner and tea every day of our lives—lunch did not feature.) The family sat

257

down to a table groaning with crackers, cutlery and enormous dishes of food, and watched as father carved the turkey at the head of the table. The meal went on for ages; we kept eating till we thought we would burst. It was wonderful. After the pudding, the grown-ups might finish off with a glass of QC port, brought home with the rest of the 'special' Christmas drinks by Dad on Christmas Eve. Wine never figured—just bottled beer and strange things with names like Cinzano and Advocaat. Then we'd all retreat to the living room to watch the Queen's speech on TV, and the grown-ups would have a nap while we kids played with our new presents till it was time to cut the Christmas cake and enjoy a slice with a cup of tea and some mince pies. Cold turkey sandwiches and stuffing came later on if you could find any room.

In the evening, there'd be board games (usually snakes and ladders or ludo), cards and charades—it wasn't polite to turn the TV on when you had visitors, even if you'd wanted to. The adults would celebrate with a glass of one of those special drinks reserved for large family get-togethers. Babycham (which was advertised as being 'champagne perry', really just a sort of cider made with pears) was the sophisticated drink for younger women since it was drunk out of its own special wide, shallow, champagne-style glasses, while the aunts might have had a port and lemon or—rather daringly—a snowball (Advocaat and fizzy lemonade) or a Cherry B—a sort of sickly cherry brandy. Men usually stuck to beer, which in those days they had to get from an off-licence at the back of a pub where you took your own jug. Bottled beer could be bought there or from the off-licence at the corner of our street that sold everything from Wincarnis tonic wine to Mackeson milk stout. What with all the fun and games and grown-ups making merry, we were allowed to stay up late. On Boxing Day we always went round to Grandma Titchmarsh's house for another big family bash with all the aunts, uncles and cousins. It was a tricky one this, since her cooking was a bit . . . well, let's just say she'd cooked her way through two World Wars, and it showed. But then it was straight back to work and normal daily life next day; Christmas was only a two-day holiday, and that was your lot till the next bank holiday at Easter.

Eating out

Eating out wasn't something people did much when I was growing up, and then it was only partaken of on special occasions such as birthdays and wedding anniversaries. If you'd gone out to eat just because you simply couldn't be bothered to cook for yourself you'd have been regarded as someone who threw their money about, and nobody wanted to be thought 'a bit flash'. What's more, only adults ate out. Parents didn't take children to restaurants. It wasn't that we didn't know how to behave because we did; it was because eating out was a big expense and a special experience that adults felt children wouldn't appreciate. For much the same reasons, when parents first started to discover foreign holidays, the children usually stayed with relatives while the adults went off on their own.

So let's suppose you'd wanted to go out to eat, 50-odd years ago; where would you go? The choice was very limited. There were no wine bars or pub grub, only hotel dining rooms (which, as now, were open to non-residents) and proper restaurants on high streets in the centres of towns. There were a few chains of steak houses such as Berni Inns, and the first hamburger chains such as Wimpy were just starting to appear—they came as quite a revelation and even they were originally sit-down restaurants with waitress service and a tomato-shaped bottle of sauce on every table. There was no question of takeaway meals or buying something to walk along eating in the street. 'The American way of eating' was a long way off yet.

Once you'd sat down at your table, you'd be given a menu. It was pretty much the same wherever you went. The most fashionable food when eating out in the fifties and early sixties was prawn cocktail (a few spoonfuls of frozen prawns with a pink sauce made by mixing tomato ketchup with salad cream, dropped into a glass filled with an *awful lot* of shredded lettuce), usually followed by steak and chips, though you could if you'd wanted choose chops, sole or some sort of pie instead. For afters you'd probably order Black Forest gateau, or perhaps an ice cream with sarsaparilla or some sweet sticky liqueur poured over the top. And to end the meal you might have an Irish coffee—black coffee in a tall glass with a dash of Irish whiskey and double cream floating on the top—which was considered the height of sophistication. It's most unlikely you'd have ordered wine with your meal, but had you been daring enough to do so it would have been a bottle of Blue Nun or Mateus rosé. My parents' first bottle of wine, which they then continued to order for most meals, was Sauternes. They graduated from that to Barsac, and then to

260

Crown of Crowns Liebfraumilch.

If you went out to lunch accompanied by children (and it would have been a very special treat), you'd go to a Wimpy Bar or the restaurant above a cinema before seeing the afternoon showing of a film. They did small portions at half price, and for pudding they'd offer a knickerbocker glory—a tall sundae glass with tinned fruit in the bottom filled to overflowing with ice cream. It was a struggle to eat the lot, but you were out for a treat and to prove it you needed to feel full to the brim or, as my wife's granny put it, BTUW—back teeth under water.

Foreign food

The only time most British people had ever been abroad, when I was a lad, was when they'd served in the armed forces during the War. Not surprisingly, they didn't look back on the experience with fond memories, and any local food they'd encountered was generally dismissed as 'filthy foreign muck' which they certainly didn't want to eat back home. It was well known that Johnny Foreigner ate things we didn't in this country (horses and donkeys, for instance), not to mention parts of the animals that a decent British family butcher wouldn't even display in their window. In any case, foreign food reeked of garlic and was swimming in olive oil, which at the time we could only buy in chemist shops to use for medicinal purposes. It's hardly surprising we Brits were conservative eaters, always suspicious of anything we'd never met before, as we'd spent many years cut off from outside supplies, existing on a very limited, bland range of wartime food.

It wasn't really until the early 1960s when daring holidaymakers started taking budget package holidays abroad that foreign food started to enter our way of life. Spain was the first big foreign holiday destination, and Benidorm on the Costa del Sol came top. Here tourists met paella and the huge irregularly shaped Continental tomatoes covered with bumps and green patches. They came as quite a culture shock to people used to the identical round red globes that you grew at home or bought from the market, weighing in at five or six to the pound. Continental tomatoes might be hideously ugly, but they were certainly packed with flavour. And anywhere you went, the food was laden with herbs, especially the Mediterranean favourites, thyme, rosemary, basil and oregano, so we started using them at home. (Up till then a sprig of mint cooked with a saucepan full of new potatoes or a bit of parsley sauce on steamed fish was about as experimental as we got with herbs.)

Italy introduced us to real spaghetti that came in long strands with a rich meaty sauce, instead of the soggy stuff that came in tins of tomato sauce to put on toast for a quick meal at home instead of baked beans. And if you ventured as far as Greece, you'd try moussaka, stuffed peppers, fried aubergines and—horror of horrors—*octopus*, which, earlier the same day, you'd probably seen a fisherman bashing against the side of the quay to tenderize it.

Naturally you had to be careful. Anything raw that you ate on the Continent—salads or fresh fruit such as grapes, figs or peaches—was automatically regarded as a health hazard. Well, you couldn't be sure if foreigners washed their hands properly— vegetables were rumoured to be grown with human sewage used as manure—and you couldn't rely on the tap water being drinkable, so even washing under the tap wouldn't render it safe. Tourists who'd booked into self-catering accommodation were advised to take plenty of permanganate of potash to rinse fresh fruit and salads, and, if you were eating out, you were advised to stick to food that had been very thoroughly cooked. Naturally you'd have to pack plenty of gippy-tummy remedies and always boil the water—even for cleaning your teeth. No wonder Mum was put off the idea of going abroad with two kids, and that's why we spent our holidays in Blackpool. You knew where you stood.

But what with worrying about the water, the unusual food and the strange local customs, and fending off sunburn and the attentions of amorous suntanned strangers, the big attraction of foreign holidays for most Brits was the way it introduced us to booze. On holiday abroad tourists could knock back cheap wine with meals, have a rum and coke afterwards, or just sit in a bar all day slugging down beers, when back home Britain was still lumbered with tight licensing hours and pubs whose landladies said 'time gentlemen please', gave you ten minutes' drinking-up time, then chucked you out. But today you can thank those early package tours for your exotic taste in food, your glass of wine after work and the gradual loosening of our stiff upper lips.

We even got used to Indian and Chinese restaurants opening over here. My dad was particularly enamoured of the first Chinese that opened in Ilkley in the early 1960s. 'They do a good meal,' he said. 'Very reasonable and lots of it.'

'What did you have?' I asked.

'Mixed grill and pear Belle Hélène,' he said. 'I like Chinese food.'

CHAPTER 10

THE WAY WE WERE AS LOYAL SUBJECTS

A few words about the royal family makes a fitting finale to this book since their presence was everywhere when I was growing up. The Queen's head appeared prominently on all our coins, banknotes and postage stamps—it wasn't cramped into a tiny corner or reduced to a silhouette as you see it today. You'd see an official portrait of the Queen in full regalia on the wall in public buildings and behind the desks of anyone from the mayor to school headmasters, and pictures of her and the royal family were on show in a good many homes. Royal news, such as engagements, births or deaths, and highlights of overseas tours, were always major stories on radio and TV and guaranteed to sell newspapers and magazines. And state occasions such as the Coronation produced floods of special issues to be carefully folded away in chocolate boxes and kept for decades along with photo albums in the family archives up in the attic. Souvenir mugs and plates were snapped up—some people collected a full set each time new ones were issued to commemorate special events, but Coronation mugs were the perennial favourites. Parks, ships and public buildings, such as hospitals, were named Queen Elizabeth after her, and so was the delightful and healthy pink rose that we still grow today.

You'd also hear 'God Save the Queen' several times every day. The national anthem was always played at the end of cinema and theatre

265

The Radio Times *listed a full week's-
worth of special Coronation broadcasting
on the BBC.*

performances. Everyone stood respectfully to attention with their heads bowed until the final strains had died away, and quite a few sang along. Everyone knew the words, from primary school age upwards, though knowledge of the second verse was generally restricted to those who had been Scouts or Guides. There was no rushing off before it was over, unless it meant missing the last bus home. The national anthem also marked the end of the night's TV broadcasts, known as close-down in the schedules, just before the picture shrank down to a small white dot that finally went out, leaving the screen blank until the test card appeared. And BBC radio stations began and ended their days broadcasting with the national anthem. (There was no 24-hour radio and TV; well, people had to get up in the morning to go to work.) No formal dinner was complete without the Loyal Toast at the end, and at home the head of the household would raise a glass to the Queen at the end of a dinner party or Christmas dinner, and she'd invariably be mentioned in prayers, in church, at school assemblies, and in private at home. Little children were especially diligent about it.

The royal family was very much loved, and they were regular topics of conversation in homes and high streets, but they always kept a certain distance between themselves and their subjects. It was the constitutional commentator Walter Bagehot who opined: 'We must not let daylight in upon the magic.' Some might feel that daylight has now flooded into the palace more than any other corner of the land.

In the 1950s you never felt that the royals were 'one of us', rather their formality and the strict protocol surrounding them all helped to maintain the aura of royal mystique that kept them special. Politicians might come and go and governments change, but the Queen and the royal family were always there—through wars, crisis and financial hardship—as a national centrepiece that linked the country together and gave us all something to look up to. In terms of the nation, their history was our history and their troubles, our troubles. They might not actually *rule* the country any more (I was rather disappointed to learn at school that they didn't still have the power to chop off heads, throw people in the Tower and confiscate stately homes, like Henry VIII did), but to a small boy it felt as if in some strange way they were the parents of the nation— wise, fair, non-judgemental and discreetly 'in the know' so you couldn't get away with anything, but they'd never let you down.

A bit of royal family history

We all think we know all about them, but here's a schoolboy's résumé for those who want a quick refresher course in how we came to be where we are. The British monarchy is the oldest in Europe, with over a thousand years of traditions and history behind it. It's a hereditary job. Queen Elizabeth II is the fortieth monarch to rule us since William the Conqueror, and her ancestry can be traced right back to Egbert, who was King of England from 827 to 839. She is a great-great-great-grandchild of Queen Victoria.

Now, it's a curious thing, but during those thousand years or so all of our most prosperous times have occurred when there's been a female monarch on the throne. Under Queen Elizabeth I and Queen Victoria the country thrived and invested heavily in buildings, science and new technology (think of the great country houses built in Elizabeth I's reign, and the railways, factories, plumbing and flush loos in Victoria's time) and that meant rising living standards and greater prosperity for their subjects. Under Elizabeth II we've seen another huge leap forward—if you think today's credit-crunch times are hard, just compare daily life today with that of your grandparents.

But what's really curious is that our present Queen should never have been Queen at all. It came about due to what was probably the biggest royal scandal our parents lived through: the abdication of King Edward VIII who gave up the throne, on 12 December 1936, for the woman he loved.

To say the nation was shocked was an understatement. For over a thousand years British kings and queens had fought, murdered and charmed their way to the throne when the lineage was uncertain, but never before had someone with a clear-cut right to the role turned it down voluntarily. Not least over a woman. But if it hadn't been for Wallis Simpson, Elizabeth, daughter of the Duke and Duchess of York and niece of King Edward VIII, would never have been Queen, and who knows how different history might have been. The abdication was still being talked about while I was small, and it had huge ramifications—not least of which was a stampede of people buying their first television set to watch the Coronation of Elizabeth II.

This—for those who were looking out of the window instead of listening in history lessons at school—is briefly what happened. When King George V died, his eldest son Edward, the Prince of Wales (known as David within the family), was the rightful successor to the throne. But he was in love with an American divorcee, Wallis Simpson, and protocol decreed that the heir could not marry someone who'd been married before, so he had to choose between the love of his life and the throne. Deciding that he couldn't live without her, he abdicated shortly before he was due to have been crowned. His younger brother Prince Albert ('Bertie') automatically moved up a notch in the royal succession and instead of being in second place, he now took pole position, and as a mark of respect for his father (George V) Prince

269

THE ILLUSTRATED

LONDON NEWS,

The World Copyright of all the Editorial Matter, both Illustrations and Letterpress, is strictly Reserved in Great Britain, the British Dominions and Colonies, Europe, and the United States of America.

SATURDAY, DECEMBER 12, 1936.

THE CONSTITUTIONAL CRISIS: HIS MAJESTY KING EDWARD VIII., WHO RAISED THE QUESTION OF A MORGANATIC MARRIAGE WHEN TALKING WITH MR. BALDWIN SOME WEEKS AGO.

The general public became aware of the constitutional crisis when they read their morning papers on Thursday, December 3. In fact, it had existed well before that. Making a statement in the House on the 7th, Mr. Baldwin said : " With the exception of the question of morganatic marriage, no advice has been tendered by the Government to his Majesty. . . . These matters were not raised first by the Government, but by his Majesty himself in conversation with me some weeks ago, when he first informed me of his intention to marry Mrs. Simpson whenever she should be free."—[B.B.C. Cameraman Photographs.]

When Prince Edward abdicated the throne in 1936, the coronation that had been planned for him went ahead instead with his younger brother, Albert, who became George VI.

Albert used his fourth Christian name, George. The Coronation that had already been planned for Edward went ahead on schedule, on 12 May 1937, but simply with a different King—George VI.

The new King was already married, to Lady Elizabeth Bowes-Lyon, and they had two children, Elizabeth and Margaret. As the elder child of the reigning King, this immediately made the elder child—Elizabeth Alexandra Mary Windsor—the heir to the throne. She was 11 at the time, and the relatively carefree life she'd led till then changed straight away, and she began a long monarchy apprenticeship. To the rest of us it seemed as if she led a fairy-tale existence—private tutors, a nanny, ponies, wonderful holidays and travel—but it was all geared to a serious purpose. She was being trained by her father for a lifetime of duty and public service. He brought her up to get on with the job whatever happened, to maintain the dignity of majesty and—most important—*not to show her emotions*. In those days the stiff upper lip prevailed, and that went for royals more than anyone.

Everything the young Princess Elizabeth did attracted media attention. She was very photogenic, and even though the general public never knew what went on behind closed palace doors, we were let in on the most glamorous, newsworthy bits. And few news stories were followed with more interest than a budding royal romance. In her teens, Princess Elizabeth fell in love with a dashing naval officer, Prince Philip of Greece, who himself was a great-great grandson of Queen Victoria. Despite his title, he wasn't what you'd call a 'working royal' as his family had been exiled from their own country since the time he was 18 months old.

Their wedding took place on 20 November 1947 at Westminster Abbey, and as far as most people were concerned it was the best thing to happen since the end of the War. A glamorous occasion was just what everyone needed to take their minds off the shortages and rationing that were still in place. More good news was to come when the heir to the throne, Prince Charles, was born on 14 November 1948, followed soon after by his sister Princess Anne in August 1950. Things seemed rosy.

But the King, who had been unwell for a while, grew steadily more ill, and early in 1952, poor health forced him to pull out of his planned state visit to Australia and New Zealand, so Princess Elizabeth and her husband stood in for him. Their first stop en route was Kenya where, after a few days of official engagements, the couple had a short holiday at Treetops, a safari-camp tree house with fabulous views over the surrounding wildlife. It was here, on 6 February 1952, that the Princess received the news that her father had died and she immediately returned home for the funeral. Shortly afterwards, at the age of 25, she was crowned Queen.

Her Coronation took place at Westminster Abbey on Tuesday 2 June 1953. It was a damp, drizzly sort of day, but a million people lined the streets of London to watch the procession, complete with marching bands, uniforms, horses and golden coach, and a good many of them had slept there overnight to be sure of their place. A staggering 27 million people watched the proceedings live on TV; a lot of people bought a set especially. Families who had a television were descended on by all their friends and neighbours who came round to watch this very special occasion, and afterwards the celebrations continued outside at street parties which were held all round the country. Red, white and blue bunting hung from houses, Union Flags were flying everywhere, and food was piled up on trestle tables. Kids could scoff all they liked. To cap it all, only the day before, news had come through that Everest had been conquered by Edmund Hillary and Sherpa Tenzing. I was only four at the time, but it made you proud to be British.

After Elizabeth became Queen her mother took the title of Queen Elizabeth the Queen Mother and moved out of Buckingham Palace to her new home in Clarence House. Royal-watchers—and most of us were in those days—followed a succession of highlights unfolding in the new Queen's life. There were royal tours. An essential stopping-off point on one of the very first was to Tonga. During the Coronation procession Queen Salote of Tonga had made a big hit with the crowds because, despite the rain, which had other VIPs closing the roof of their carriages, she'd kept the top of hers open so the crowds could see her. She was so taken by London and her rapturous welcome that she issued an invitation to the young Queen and Prince Philip to visit Tonga, and when they arrived they were driven round in the London taxi that she'd taken back home with her after the Coronation. A huge feast was laid on for the royal couple, which turned out to be a glorified barbecue for 700 people, all eating roast suckling pig, yams and other local delicacies with their fingers. This posed a little problem of protocol, since being the person of highest rank present, everyone else had to stop eating when the

273

Queen did, so she diplomatically stretched out her meal to let her fellow guests take their fill—she was always a small eater.

Meanwhile the Queen's younger sister, Princess Margaret, attracted plenty of media attention of her own. She was known as a great party-girl, and newspapers followed her love life with particular interest. The scandal-monitor rose in 1955 until she finally decided *not* to marry the divorcee Group Captain Peter Townsend after all. Meanwhile the Queen's family increased; Prince Andrew was born in 1960 and Prince Edward in 1964. More good royal news came in a steady stream. First Princess Margaret's wedding to Mr Anthony Armstrong-Jones in 1960, then the Queen launching the *QE2* (which was named after her) in 1967 at Clydebank. Nineteen sixty-nine saw Prince Charles invested as Prince of Wales at Caernarvon Castle, as well as doing his *Goon Show* impression for a student review at Cambridge University, and in 1973 we had the first royal wedding that most of us children of the 1950s remember—that of Princess Anne to Captain Mark Phillips.

In between these notable occasions we saw regular shots in the news of the royal family enjoying themselves at Royal Ascot (both the Queen and the Queen Mother were successful racehorse owners and breeders), Prince Charles playing polo and Princess Anne showjumping, the family going to church at Sandringham or up to Balmoral for Christmas, or simply as a family group surrounded by a sea of ever-present corgis, besides being 'on duty' in their official capacities. There was very little of what you'd call royal scandal-mongering, gossip or speculation; apart from carefully rehearsed and stage-managed public events and limited official shots of the young royal family growing up, we were rarely, if ever, allowed glimpses behind the scenes. The royal family was still special and shrouded in mystery, so any chance to see them gave the man in the street a thrill.

Today people often think the Queen's role is mostly as a tourist attraction, but there's a lot more to it than that. The power of our monarchy has certainly been eroded over the centuries since the British Civil War when Charles I was executed for being perceived as a bad King, and Parliament—which represented the people—grew stronger by leaps and bounds. But at least—unlike the rest of Europe—we've kept our royal family as heads of state, which gives a great feeling of tradition and continuity. As one wag remarked: 'In fifty years' time there will be only five royal families remaining: Hearts, Clubs, Diamonds, Spades and Windsor.'

Today we have what's known as a 'constitutional monarchy', which means a lot of ceremonial roles but no real power—just the position to oil diplomatic and political wheels. The Queen can influence and advise using her lifetime's experience gained from dealings with a dozen different Prime Ministers, starting with Winston Churchill. Whether she is making a royal visit at home or abroad, welcoming visiting heads of state to receptions at Buckingham Palace or dispensing honours at investiture ceremonies, she is always knowledgeable about the people she meets and the places she visits, thanks to a vast network of Palace and diplomatic staff who keep her well briefed. But although it's the Queen we always think of in connection with royal duties, it's a family firm—the Duke of Edinburgh, the Prince of Wales, the Princess Royal and other immediate members of the royal family all do their bit, often in the face of stern criticism. And yet, even the most hardened and cynical critics, on meeting the monarch, can be reduced to jelly. I know. I've seen 'em.

The job

Oh, there's a common perception that the Queen just opens things, and her working life is all chauffeured limousines, red carpets and the smell of fresh paint, but when you look into it there's a lot more to it. Hers is a multifaceted role, and amid the glamour and excitement, there's dogged determination, a fair amount of tedium and a lot of routine paperwork.

On the political front, the monarch's role is to officially appoint the Prime Minister after a general election, and invite him or her to form a government. The Queen presides over the State Opening of Parliament, when she travels to the House of Lords in the famous Golden Coach and sends her representative Black Rod to the House of Commons to summon the MPs. (As a traditional gesture of defiance, the MPs always slam the door in Black Rod's face the first time he knocks.) Then when the MPs have crammed into the House of Lords, the Queen—in full regalia complete with a very heavy crown—reads her Government's plans for the forthcoming session, and then travels back to the Palace. She meets with the Prime Minister once a week, on a Tuesday evening, to discuss events in complete confidence, and in the summer when she's at Balmoral in Scotland the PM travels up with his wife and combines the weekly meeting with an overnight visit. When a PM steps down, he must ask the Queen for permission to resign.

There's a large religious side to the role; the Queen is 'Defender of the Faith', heading up the Church of England, and as such she helps to give the country moral and spiritual leadership. Wherever she is in the world, she goes to church each Sunday. When she took the throne Britain was still a strongly Christian country, small children went to Sunday school, a lot of us sang in church choirs or became bell-ringers, and the school day always started with a small act of worship at morning assembly. Now that we have a multicultural, multifaith society, the Queen is careful to cover all angles and avoid offending anyone. This is particularly true for her Christmas message on TV, which goes out to the whole Commonwealth as well as those of us sitting at home in Blighty, stuffed to the gills with turkey and plum pudding. The Queen made her first Christmas broadcast in 1952, before her Coronation, and it's been a regular part of family Christmases ever since. She doesn't jump up from her Christmas dinner at Sandringham to do it 'live'—it's recorded slightly in advance and broadcast alternately by the BBC and ITV.

Much of the Queen's role is to act as a sort of official patter-of-backs, on a grand scale. State awards for high achievement are announced twice a year with the publication of the honours list, one on New Year's Eve and the other on her official birthday in June. The recipients of the decorations are selected by a network of various organizations including the Government of the day—they can

THE TRADITION OF
MAUNDY MONEY

At Easter the Queen and her retinue move to Windsor for a month. (This is the family home, since Buckingham Palace is more like 'the office' where they sleep over the shop, and Balmoral and Sandringham are really holiday homes.) But before moving to Windsor, the Queen undertakes an ancient tradition—that of giving out Maundy Money, on Maundy Thursday, the day before Good Friday.

In medieval times Maundy Thursday was the day the monarch humbled himself (or herself) by selecting a group of poor people, feeding and clothing them, then washing their feet and giving them alms. Successive monarchs made minor modifications to the old tradition; foot-washing was dropped due to the risk of infection when the plague was rife, and from James II onwards the whole ceremony was reduced to a straightforward cash donation dispensed by the monarch's representative. Our current Queen's grandfather King George V did the job himself on just one occasion, and her father King George VI did it a few times, but the Queen took to the idea and revived the Maundy ceremony in its present form some 40 years ago; she now does it every year at a different cathedral.

The beneficiaries of Maundy Money are no longer the poor: they are a mixture of people chosen for their contribution to community life, one man and one woman for each year of the Queen's life. During the ceremony, the specially minted Maundy Money is carried in a procession on huge gold dishes by Yeomen of the Guard wearing Tudor uniform. After a brief service the cathedral choir sings something suitably soaring, and each of the recipients is given a red purse containing £5.50 and a white purse containing one penny for each year of the sovereign's life. (The coins are worth far more to collectors than their face value, but they are very rarely sold.)

All that's left of the foot-washing business are the towels and bags of herbs carried by the Queen's attendants. Her Majesty must be quite relieved.

even be nominated by the general public. Years ago it was mostly all retiring civil servants, diplomats, military men, captains of industry and similar worthies who were nominated for honours, but as life loosened up all sorts of people were given 'gongs'—The Beatles were awarded MBEs in 1965, which prompted a flood of people sending theirs back in disgust. Nowadays the names on the list can include newsreaders, soap stars, Olympic athletes, road sweepers and milkmen. A very few top honours are the Queen's to award as she wishes; the orders of the Garter, the Thistle, the Royal Victorian Order and the Order of Merit. Each honours list contains roughly 1,300 names, and while the Queen used to present all the awards herself at investiture ceremonies in the Ballroom at Buckingham Palace, she now shares the job with the Prince of Wales and the Princess Royal. Some investitures are held at Windsor Castle, as well as at Holyrood House in Edinburgh.

The royal garden parties are another way of recognizing people who have done something for the country or their community; each summer the Queen holds three for 8,000 people a time at Buckingham Palace, and another one for 10,000 at Holyrood Palace in Edinburgh, where the royal family spend a week every summer. At each of these she'll probably manage to meet and speak to about 200 people personally, but it's a huge honour to be invited and all sorts of people can find themselves on the guest list—long-standing school dinner ladies can easily find themselves munching shortbread or queueing up for their cuppa in the tea tent along with ambassadors and their wives. And even though you'd wonder how she knows, centenarians still get a birthday card from the Queen (it's no longer a telegram), and so do couples who reach their 75th (diamond) wedding anniversary.

Royal visits fall into two camps. There are the huge state visits, of which she'll do two or three a year, which take six months of planning and may cover several countries or even continents. But the majority of royal visits are short; she'll often do five or six a day, to events at schools, factories and charitable events of all sorts. Her presence always ensures plenty of media coverage. Between them, the Queen and the rest of the royal family support 3,500 charitable organizations; there's nothing like a royal patron or president for raising the profile of a good cause. Royal visits of this type are also made by all 13 members of the royal family who receive an income from the Civil List; between them they undertake 4,000 visits each year. The Princess Royal alone fulfils over 600 such engagements, and the Prince of Wales almost as many. (There are also armies of people including Lord Lieutenants—one for each county—who represent the Queen at occasions such as memorial services that she cannot attend personally.) Over a year, it's been reckoned that half a million people will have had some sort of encounter with one or other of the royal family. Royal engagements are collated by the relevant department at the Palace and sent to all the newspapers daily, so they can decide which they want to cover; one or two of the quality newspapers still print a 'Court Circular' column so that curious readers can see what the Queen and major royals are up to, though for security reasons it only tells you the previous day's itinerary. Even so it makes fascinating reading.

The military play a big part in the royal family's activities. The Queen is Commander-in-Chief of all our armed forces, who swear to serve 'Queen and country'. She has seven regiments to guard her, which are known collectively as the Household Division. These are the colourful guardsmen that tourists love to watch on duty outside Buckingham Palace on horseback or wearing red uniforms and bearskins and taking part in the daily changing of the guards ceremony. The Household Division is made up of two mounted regiments—the Household Cavalry (the Lifeguards and the Blues and Royals) and the foot guards, who consist of the Grenadier Guards, the Coldstream Guards, the Scots Guards, the Irish Guards and the Welsh Guards. Despite their traditional ceremonial role, soldiers from these units also take turns doing tours of duty overseas in war zones, just like other soldiers, so it's not all pomp and ceremony.

The Queen is involved with two military events that always make a big splash on TV: Remembrance Day at the Cenotaph and Trooping the Colour. Remembrance Day always takes place on the second Sunday in November, and it's the day Britain honours its war dead. The crowds gather round the Cenotaph, in Whitehall, the Queen takes her place, then the Royal Artillery fires a single shot to sound the start of the two minutes' silence (which is observed all round the country) and a second one at the end, after which the Queen lays her wreath followed by the Prime Minister and a succession of other VIPs. Then there's a service and the national anthem, followed by a march-past by veteran soldiers, sailors and airmen in uniforms weighed down by medals, some of whom have to be pushed along in wheelchairs. There are usually around 10,000 of them, including the Chelsea Pensioners from the Royal Hospital. It's a very solemn and moving occasion.

Trooping the Colour is an ancient ceremony that was originally established to show the 'colours' (basically their regimental flag) to soldiers so they'd recognize their own side in the thick of a battle, but these days it's more of a tribute from the Household Division to celebrate the Queen's official birthday. The ceremony takes place on the first Saturday in June at Horse Guards Parade; the Queen and other members of the royal family set out from the Palace in a procession of horses and carriages. The Queen always used to ride side-saddle—latterly on her favourite horse Burmese, but when Burmese was retired in 1986 the Queen switched to a carriage pulled by a pair of Windsor greys instead. On arrival the Queen takes her seat in the parade chair at one end of the grounds, then the troops march past, bands playing, 'colour' carried, then she goes back to the Palace at the head of a procession of her soldiers. Once there she watches the troops march past again, then goes into the Palace, where the family and far-flung members who've arrived for the party are gathered in the big room behind the balcony, in time to see the Royal Artillery fire the salute of cannon in Hyde Park. Then it's out onto the balcony to watch the RAF fly-past and wave to the crowds before going back inside for a big family lunch.

The royal household is run by a huge staff. At its head is the Lord Chamberlain, whose duties once included the onerous task of censoring films before they were passed fit for public viewing; no sooner was this role dropped in the mid-sixties than our stages and screens were struck by a tide of full-frontal nudity and four-letter words. (Anyone who was around at the time may still remember the fuss when the rock musical *Hair* and the play *Oh Calcutta!* came to London.) The job of the Lord Chamberlain's office now is to organize ceremonial events, such as investitures and garden parties, but he also acts as liaison between the Queen and the various departments that make up her staff. The Master of the Household is the chap who actually *runs* the royal household with a staff of more than 200, who do all the cleaning and cooking—including preparations for big occasions such as banquets—all to the very highest standards. The Queen often entertains heads of state visiting

283

Britain from other countries, and they are given the full works—involving legendary precision in organizational skills and attention to detail. A carriage procession down the Mall to the Palace is only the start. When the procession arrives the visitors will be moved into a guest suite with their retinue being put up in adjacent guest rooms, followed by lunch and the exchange of official and personal gifts, then there'll be a state banquet the same night and a royal send-off after breakfast next morning.

There's the press office for media requests and enquiries, and the information office that looks after the royal website and sends out the daily list of royal activities. The ladies-in-waiting have an office; they help the Queen with her huge correspondence from her subjects (she reads as many of them herself as she can, but every letter is answered, almost always by a lady-in-waiting), and they act as companions on royal visits, carrying the flowers and gifts she is given. The private secretary's office organizes the Queen's engagement diary and helps plan official visits for the whole royal family; the travel office makes the necessary arrangements for journeys by royal train, boat, car, helicopter or plane (there are actually seven planes, of various sizes, but they aren't all kept just for her personal use—for the sake of economy they are shared with cabinet ministers). There's the treasurer's office which looks after the finances, and another department that takes care of the royal collections, which include valuable paintings and antique furniture belonging to the crown which is passed on from one generation to another. It's not surprising that of the 650-ish rooms inside Buckingham Palace, most are offices, with guest suites and the royal apartments taking up only one wing. And despite the staff of hundreds attending to everything in meticulous detail, the Queen herself checks, inspects and approves one heck of a lot of it personally, especially the plans for banquets—right down to the flowers.

As if that wasn't enough, wherever the Queen travels, at 7pm every evening she takes delivery of a red box stuffed full of papers to be read and inwardly digested, and documents to sign. The box will also contain briefings on the people and places she is to visit, which is why she is always so well informed; there'll also be a concise account of the day in Parliament, and weekly summaries from Governor-Generals of other countries of which she is Queen. She'll have been through them all before breakfast next morning. At weekends there's a double dose. As jobs go, there's no let-up. She's rarely 'off duty'.

As time has marched on we've seen a series of divorces in the royal family, the tragedy of Princess Diana's death and the remarriage of the heir to the throne, and we've been let into their private lives more closely than ever thanks to countless TV documentaries, biographies and scandalous revelations in the press. But when you look at how much society has changed in the time since Elizabeth II became Queen, it's remarkable that she has managed to retain the affection, the loyalty and the respect of the vast majority of her subjects. She alone has done a tremendous job in upholding the standards and traditions that those of us born in the first half of the twentieth century might have expected to have been swept aside. Hers has been a life of great privilege, undeniably, but more importantly it has been one of duty and service—two words which, for most of us now, seem at best quaint and at worst old fashioned—along with their dictionary companions loyalty, discretion, modesty and respect.

Since I grew up, we've seen technology put computers on everyone's desk and fill homes with more entertainment media, kitchen gadgets and power tools than we'd ever have thought possible. We've seen living standards rise and disposable income shoot up. Quite ordinary families now run several cars, take foreign holidays and eat food that would have been unthinkable when I was a boy, so compared to everyday life for normal families in the 1950s and 1960s we live like kings. The monarchy has changed too—we've glimpsed, from time to time, their feet of clay; their everyday actions are the stuff of the tabloids. They now get out of their cars and go on walkabouts, market their own products, run royal farmshops and pay income tax like the rest of us, but in spite of all this they've never lost the ability to dazzle, to charm and to lend a regal air to any occasion, which still makes us the envy of the world. They give us a bit of 'special', and however much technology advances and standards fall, we all need a little sparkle in our lives. It lifts us out of the spiritual mire and gives us, for one brief shining moment, a much-needed shot of optimism. We may have lost some of our post-war prudence, and times have certainly changed for all of us, but behind it all our national character has much to commend it, as times of stress and tragedy occasionally remind us. Our ability to laugh at ourselves, to buckle down when we have to and 'to do the right thing' may not be quite as much in evidence as they were during the War, but they are qualities that are still at the heart of the British character, and long may they remain so.

PICTURE CREDITS

The author and publisher gratefully acknowledge the permission granted to reproduce the copyright material in this book. Every effort has been made to trace copyright holders and to obtain their permission for the use of copyright material. The publisher apologizes for any errors or omissions in the list below and would be grateful if notified of any corrections that should be incorporated in future reprints or editions of this book.

Integrated pictures Photographs supplied by Alan Titchmarsh and © Alan Titchmarsh: 4, 117, 208. © Alamy: 22. BBC: 212, 213, 223, 224. Mary Evans Picture Library: 91, 107, 137, 249, 256

Plate section Page 1 (both) Alan Titchmarsh; 2 (bottom) Mary Evans Picture Library; 3 (bottom) Mary Evans Picture Library; 4 (top and bottom) Alamy; 5 (top) Mary Evans Picture Library; 6 (both) Mary Evans Picture Library; 7 (both) Mary Evans Picture Library; 8 (top) Alan Titchmarsh, (bottom) Mary Evans Picture Library; 9 (both) Mary Evans Picture Library; 10 (top and top right) Alamy; 11 (top) Mary Evans Picture Library; 12 (both) Alan Titchmarsh; 13 (bottom) Mary Evans Picture Library; 15 (top left) Alamy, (top right) Mary Evans Picture Library; 16 (middle right) Alamy, (bottom) Mary Evans Picture Library.

ACKNOWLEDGEMENTS

I am tremendously grateful to Caroline McArthur for her endless editorial patience and persistence, to Wendy Smith for her assiduous copy editing, Sue Phillips for her painstaking research and Claire Gouldstone for seeking out appropriate images to illustrate the nineteen-fifties backwater that was my childhood. This is not so much a memoir as a reflection on how life was just after the war and before the advent of the 'Swinging Sixties'—although I've inevitably slid into them on occasions. There were times when I felt that 'surely everybody knows this', and some readers who are my contemporaries may feel the same. But perhaps they will enjoy the triggered memories of their childhood, and my recollections might make an amusing document for those who were not around back then and who wonder how we filled our days. Lorna Russell kept me going and offered encouragement when I most needed it. She and the other ladies in my literary life deserve my thanks.